BUILDING MORAL COMMUNITIES

A GUIDE FOR EDUCATORS

MICHAEL SCHULMAN, PH.D.

The Council for Spiritual and Ethical Education
www.csee.org

D1510982

BUILDING MORAL COMMUNITIES: A GUIDE FOR EDUCATORS
by Michael Schulman

ISBN: 0-9778934-0-5

Copies of this and other CSEE publications may be purchased through
The Council for Spiritual and Ethical Education
See purchase and contact information at www.csee.org

Cover design by Kara M. Mansfield Morehouse
Annie Warner and Julie Stevens also contributed to the publication of this work

Published by the Council for Spiritual and Ethical Education
March 2006

CONTENTS

About the Author

PREFACE

This book presents a framework and guide for bringing moral instruction into our schools. It starts from the premise that schools are communities, and that for moral education to succeed in a school setting, the school must be recreated as a moral community. The central goal of a moral community is to establish a culture of caring to counter the cultures of selfishness, exclusion, and violence in which many young people grow up. The recommendations herein cover many aspects of school operations, from school-wide administrative issues, to how teachers can highlight the moral content in the standard curricula, to detailed suggestions for character education exercises.

The book is addressed to school administrators, to principals and teachers, to board members, and to any others in the school community who are seeking ways to better prepare our children to lead principled and compassionate lives. The framework offered here can, I believe, be applied to any school, but each school will have to adapt the recommendations to its own particular structure, setting, and student population. A large, urban school with a thousand or more students from diverse economic and ethnic backgrounds will confront far different issues than a selective private school or a small public school in a more affluent, relatively homogeneous suburb. Similarly, moral education for second graders will differ from moral education for high school students.

Important philosophical and political issues arise whenever schools consider taking on the responsibility of moral instruction. For instance, parents ask, "Whose morality will be taught?" and "Where does religion come in?" These and various other questions are analyzed here and it is hoped that the perspective provided can be used by school personnel to ease the concerns of parents and other community members and gain their support.

The author expresses appreciation to the University Seminars at Columbia University for their help in publication. Material in this work was presented to the Columbia University Seminar on Ethics, Moral Education, and Society.

I would also like to express my gratitude to Dr. Eva Fogelman for inviting me to write the original edition of this book, then titled *Schools as Moral Communities*, as part of an educational project of the Anti-Defamation League.

I am similarly indebted to David Streight and the Council for Spiritual and Ethical Education for the opportunity to revise and expand the original text, in order to make it available to a wider audience.

THE MORAL LIFE OF SCHOOLS

More and more schools are rediscovering that they cannot avoid moral instruction. Regardless of which curriculum or instructional format they adopt or which social atmosphere they seek to establish, their choices invariably have a significant impact on their students' moral concerns and conduct, both inside and outside the school. Increasingly, schools have been seeking ways to influence their students toward more moral choices, aspiring to help them lead more compassionate and principled lives during their school years and beyond. This program provides a format for accomplishing that goal.

Schools are complex institutions with many components and many layers of authority. The school community consists of administrators, board members, teachers, students, parents, and many types of "nonprofessional" personnel (such as secretaries, custodians, bus drivers, security guards, and lunchroom staff). Moreover, schools function within, and are beholden to, their communities at large with their various, and often competing, social and political constituencies.

A truly effective moral education program must rally and unite all the components of the community. Indeed, the goal must be to transform the school into a moral community, one in which all members feel respected and appreciated and in which all take responsibility for the school's social climate. If the school's goal is simply to find a way to get the students to behave themselves, it cannot succeed.

In the chapters that follow, we will explore the key elements required to turn schools into moral communities. No school is likely to institute everything described in this book, but all schools should keep in mind that the more comprehensive the moral education program, the greater the likelihood that it will have an impact.

CHAPTER 1

ADMINISTRATIVE ISSUES

The administration of a school is responsible for its guiding philosophy. If its goal is moral education, the school must define and declare its mission openly and affirmatively: "This school is a place that celebrates and strives to pass on the best of human civilization, covering excellence in many domains of human achievement (science, art, athletics, etc.), not the least of which is moral excellence."

The goal must be manifest for a number of reasons:

a) The administration must become an inspirational force within the school and this can only be accomplished by openly espousing morality and identifying it with excellence.

b) Since moral education will best succeed in a moral community, and since a moral community requires the contribution of all members, all must be clear about the goal. Morality often requires surrendering some immediate benefit for a deferred but greater good. Members of the school community become more willing to exert self-control when they are clear about the long term benefits of doing so.

c) The goal must also be clear because ultimately all policies and practices—from how rules are made to how rule infractions are handled—will be designed with that goal in mind. For instance, in many schools, student rule infractions are framed in terms of power and punishment, with teachers and administrators communicating, in essence, "You broke my rule. I am more powerful than you. I will punish you." In schools that are openly striving to become moral communities, power is still exercised, but only in the service of the school's noble mission—to pass on the torch of civilization to the next generation. The message to the rule breaker is then more likely to be, "We are building an environment here in which everyone has a right to feel safe and valued, because that is everyone's fundamental right in our society and because that is the only atmosphere in which children can do their best learning." Sometimes that framework will lead to reevaluating the rule that was broken, rather than reflexively punishing the transgressor.

When a school ponders its role as moral educator, certain questions invariably arise. Obviously, the most important is, Should schools take on the responsibility of moral education? Tied to this question are the issues of Which (or whose) morality should be taught? and What is the role of religion in moral instruction in a school? Another critical question is, How can we avoid the pitfalls of moral dogmatism and zealotry? Finally, we need some confidence that if we choose to teach morality, we know how to teach it—that we know the answer to the question, How do children acquire morals?

Let's look at each of these questions:

Should Schools Take On the Responsibility of Moral Education?

Actually this is a bogus question since schools cannot avoid "doing" moral education. A given school may or may not choose to do it formally or thoughtfully, but it cannot avoid doing it. For instance, if a teacher sees one boy hit another, there are many things she can do. She can display anger and impose a punishment ("You cannot go to recess!"). She can remind the offender about the rules against hitting and why they exist ("We don't allow hitting here because children can't learn and be their best if they are afraid of being hit"). She can try to stimulate empathy in him with reminders of how he felt when he was picked on. She can assert her own feelings ("It truly pains me when I see a child being hurt. No child deserves that. That's why I must prevent you from hitting another child, just as I would prevent anyone from hitting you"). She can attempt to find out what precipitated the hitting and act on that information (perhaps the boy needs to learn more constructive ways to handle conflicts, such as anger management or negotiation techniques; or perhaps his aggression was actually a byproduct of some serious family disturbance that occurred before school, in which case she might convey that he can seek help if he comes into school feeling bad but that he cannot take out his bad feelings on others).

Through her demeanor, the teacher can be rejecting of the boy's aggressive acts or she can be rejecting of the boy. She can also simply walk away and do nothing, telling herself that moral education is not her responsibility.

Each of these choices, including the last, conveys a different moral message, from "Don't hit because the adults will punish you," to "Don't hit because it undermines our noble mission as a school," to "Don't hit because it makes others feel bad," to "It's okay to hit since the adults don't do anything about it."

Obviously few teachers would take the last option and simply walk away while a child is being hit—but which of the other possible actions should she take? Since there is no way to avoid a moral message, what is the best one to impart? Moreover, should the manner of handling student disputes and infractions be left to each teacher to decide on his or her own, or should the school try to develop a consistent and thoughtful policy and prepare teachers on how to carry it out?

Since schools are in the moral education business whether they like it or not, it would seem sensible for them to accept their responsibility openly and to create a school-wide program in as thoughtful a way as they can.

The question arises, "Isn't moral education the responsibility of the child's parents or religious leaders?" The answer is obviously yes, but that doesn't eliminate the responsibility of the school. For example, if a parent teaches his child to hit back anyone who hits him ("an eye for an eye"), and the school has a policy that says don't hit back but tell the teacher, then the school is not likely to make an exception and allow this child to hit back. Within its jurisdiction the school will no doubt override the parent's directive and do its best to explain to both parent and child the moral merit of its policy (in all likelihood without using the touchy word "moral").

Similarly, if a child belongs to a religious denomination that preaches racist or sexist ideology (as some do), and if the child acts on that ideology in the school, few school authorities would simply throw up their hands and say, "We can't intervene since his religion takes precedence on moral matters."

Schools did not always shy away from moral education. Indeed, they accepted it as an inherent part of their mandate. For example, when Thomas Jefferson described his goals in founding the University of Virginia, he made clear that he believed a central aim of education is to develop virtue in students: "Education generates habits of application, of order and the love of virtue; and controls, by the force of habit, any innate obliquities in our moral organization."

There are many factors that made schools—especially public schools—cautious in recent decades about teaching morality. Morality traditionally came as a package of do's and don'ts that included obeying authorities, both secular and religious, believing in God and participating in one's religion, accepting the moral superiority of "our" (white, Euro-American) culture to others, and adhering to highly restrictive sexual codes. In the latter part of the twentieth century we began to change as a society, conceding more openly that our secular and religious leaders may not be models of morality, that belief in God does not guarantee virtue, that our ethnocentrism has blinded us to the merits of other cultures, and that sexual abstinence is not a reasonable criterion for judging whether someone is a good person.

Thus, for many people, serious doubts arose about the traditional moral package. Parents became confused about what values to teach their children. Schools, reflecting the same uncertainty, balked at teaching any values at all. "Value-free education" became the catchphrase. The most schools would do was help students clarify their values or reason "more maturely" about them, but not dare to assert that some values are better than others. This brings us to our next question.

WHICH (OR WHOSE) MORALITY SHOULD BE TAUGHT?

While many components of traditional morality have been challenged, certain core values, like kindness and fairness, continue to be widely accepted. At the heart of virtually all religious and ethical systems is the imperative to treat others kindly and fairly. We judge people as kind only if we believe that they make an effort to enhance the lives of those around them. We judge them as fair only if they strive to make sure that each person receives what he or she deserves. We judge people as moral only if we believe they try to treat others kindly and fairly.

Many other virtues derive from these core values, including honesty, sportsmanship, tolerance, respectfulness, and accepting one's responsibilities. Few would argue against teaching our children any of these.

We might differ with others over how to put these values into practice or disagree over what is fair in a given situation (Do the homeless deserve decent dwellings in decent neighborhoods or would that just reinforce their unsuccessful lifestyles and denigrate the efforts of those who have earned their way into those neighborhoods?). We might doubt the wisdom or knowledge of those who opt for different policies, but if we feel they are sincerely trying to bring about kind and fair outcomes (such as decent housing for everyone), we can still respect their moral intentions.

Concerns about *Whose morality?* don't usually arise when schools seek to foster kindness, fairness, honesty, responsibility, and similar traits. Schools have always tried to do this. Concerns will certainly arise if schools take stands on controversial policies about how to bring about moral ends. Schools that advocate liberal or conservative solutions, or openly religious or anti-religious solutions, are sure to rouse the ire of significant segments of the community. Few would disagree that it is essential and legitimate for schools to teach about the major moral debates in our society, explicating the various positions in the debate. Most would also agree that it is not the province of the school or any teacher to insist that students adopt a particular viewpoint in the controversy.

Community concerns also arise when schools take "moral" stands on issues not necessarily having to do with kindness and fairness, such as trying to define what kind of sexual behavior is permissible for students at different ages or linking morality to hair and clothing styles. These are matters of community and family conventions and personal tastes and sensibilities. They are not trivial issues, but they are not about kindness and fairness and should not be confused with the goals of a moral education program. Students know very well that there are "bad" people who follow community dress codes and have neat haircuts, and that there are good people who don't.

Sexual behavior and dress codes vary from community to community and change within communities across time, but kindness and fairness are central to every major religious and ethical system. One finds The Golden Rule, with slight variations in wording, in Christianity, Judaism, Islam, Hinduism, Buddhism, Confucianism, Taoism, and Zoroastrianism, among others. In some it is stated in positive terms ("Do unto others as you would have them do unto you"); in others it is stated in negative terms ("Do not do unto others what you would not have done to you"). But the unstated assumption in The Golden Rule is that because everyone wishes to be treated kindly and fairly, by following the rule one will treat others kindly and fairly.

What Is the Place of Religion in Moral Instruction in a School?

Kindness, fairness, honesty, responsibility and similar virtues do not need to be taught within a religious framework. As mentioned, The Golden Rule is found in all major religious and ethical systems and, in all, conveys the same message: Put yourself, heart and mind, in the place of those with whom you interact. Children do not need a religious justification to understand and appreciate the value of this message and many spontaneously show signs of concern for others even before they are three, before formal religious instruction has begun.

Some argue that religion is our only source of morality and that it is futile or even sacrilegious to teach morality outside of religion. They assert that there is no reason to be good except out of the fear or love of God. This is really an empirical question: Can people who don't believe in God be good? If "good" means strive to treat others kindly and fairly, no doubt they can.

The psychological foundations of moral motivation are independent of, but not antithetical to, the belief in a deity. Children naturally develop moral motivations and what might be called "susceptibilities" to moral instruction. By their third year many have already developed the capacity for empathy, becoming able to put themselves in another's place. And by the end of their preschool years many will have developed principles of right and wrong and the capacity to be moved and influenced by moral ideals (by visions of moral excellence). Schools can support and stimulate these capacities in a number of ways, including:

+ fostering empathy by encouraging children to take on the perspectives of others,

+ stimulating ideals by helping children develop a vision of a better world (a better school, a better community, etc.) that is truly achievable—one in which kindness and fairness prevail,

+ always trying to treat the children kindly and fairly,

+ standing strongly for kindness and fairness by insisting that the children treat each other, and other members of the school community, kindly and fairly.

All of these procedures (and others described below) foster moral motivation and none requires the justification of a deity to be effective.

Parochial and private schools are not constrained by the U.S. Constitution and laws mandating separation of church and state, but even in public schools there are ways that religion can, I believe, legitimately enter the school house. For example, I don't believe the separation clause would be violated if students were encouraged to think about how their religion wants them to treat their fellow human beings. Such discussions might take place in counseling, advisory, or values clarification sessions, but they must be done with great sensitivity. It is certainly not the school's place to use the child's religious beliefs for discipline purposes, say by suggesting that the child will be rewarded or punished by God for his or her behavior. But a school might legitimately encourage children to think about the important influences on their beliefs and attitudes, including religious influences.

A second legitimate role for religion in the schools is directly in the curriculum. Many educators and public officials of all political persuasions have noted that by sanitizing curricula of religion, teachers and textbooks have actually distorted history. One complaint has been that lessons about the Pilgrims and other groups that sought freedom in this country do not mention that it was primarily religious freedom that they were after—that many of these groups were essentially religious communities.

Our schools, trying to stay neutral with regard to religion, have, for the most part, left out of their curricula the enormous impact of religion on human cultures. Since, throughout human history, our governments, commerce, wars, migrations, morality, daily routines, art, architecture, music, and even our science have been influenced mightily by religion, this has been a significant omission.

There is a growing consensus that schools need to grant religion its rightful place in the curriculum, and I would agree. But this will not be a simple task, particularly if educators seek to avoid another form of distortion about religion. If we teach our children that Gandhi's great acts were inspired by his religious beliefs, should we not also teach them that so were the acts of the man who assassinated him?

If our goal now is to teach the truth about religion, then, along with appreciating the enormous contribution of religion to morality, we must include the fact that religion has not always been a benign influence in human affairs. Religious intolerance has been at the root of many wars, as well as the Inquisition and anti-Semitism. The same Bible that contains the Ten Commandments also condones slavery and genocide. The same religion that preaches love for one's enemy burned their enemies at the stake. Some religious groups in the U.S. and Europe denounced slavery and the slaughter of Native Americans; others defended it. Galileo was condemned by a religious edict for speaking his mind; so was Salman Rushdie. And our daily newspapers attest to the fact that atrocities committed in the name of religion are still very much with us.

If we teach about religion in human culture but leave out the negative aspects, we are instituting a new kind of distortion of the truth. Moreover, if schools are only allowed to teach about the noble and humane aspects of religion, then schools become, in effect, advocates of religion—a position our Constitution forbids. On the other hand, if schools include the negative aspects of religion, they are sure to upset influential forces in the community.

But, why teach history, including the role of religion in history, unless it is to learn from the successes and failures of our predecessors? For instance, we are a society that strongly values religious tolerance. To preserve it, we, and our children, must know about the horrible consequences of religious intolerance, even if that means pointing out the intolerance in the histories of many of our religions. If schools bring religion into their curricula, and I believe they should, they will need courage to tell the whole truth about religion, to reveal it as an institution that has inspired our most admirable and our most terrible passions.

One educational domain that I feel religion does not belong in is science class, whether the subject matter is biology, cosmology, or any other area of science. Science seeks natural (that is, spatio-temporal) explanations for natural phenomena. The supernatural explanations propounded under the rubrics "creation science" and "intelligent design" offer the same non-spatio-temporal explanation for everything: God did it. This view puts an end to inquiry. Science proceeds through theories that lead to testable hypotheses (at least conceivably testable) which predict that under such and such conditions, this or that will happen. For example, Einstein's gravitational theory predicted that massive bodies bend light waves (something no scientific or religious theory had ever imagined). It took some years before it could be tested, but when it was, the prediction was confirmed. Untestable beliefs have no place in science.

HOW CAN WE AVOID THE PITFALLS OF MORAL DOGMATISM AND ZEALOTRY?

If we bring moral education into the school we need to remember the adage, "The road to hell is paved with good intentions." The Hitler Youth and China's Red Guards are examples of youth educated to further malevolent causes in the name of a higher morality. Indeed, because some of humankind's worst atrocities have been committed under the guise of a higher morality, and because young people are so readily susceptible to moral inspiration, we must do our best to prepare them for, and inoculate them against, the seductive arguments of moral zealots.

Morality can go awry for a number of reasons. Probably the most dangerous is when moral leaders encourage us to deny full humanity to some portion of the population and exclude them from moral consideration: "They are Gypsies (or Jews or Catholics or Capitalists or Communists or Blacks or Whites or...), so we don't have to treat them well. Indeed, we are righteous when we do them harm or exterminate them." Obviously, we must prepare our children to see through and reject any depictions of "our" group and "their" group that justifies subjugating or tyrannizing other human beings.

To prevent children from adopting xenophobic attitudes, schools need to stress the achievements and common humanity of all peoples. They can do this by teaching an appreciation of different cultures, by exploring their social institutions, art, stories, and technical accomplishments, as well as their views on morality. Equally important is to teach children about the terrible consequences that have ensued when one group has dehumanized another and denied moral status to its members. The lessons of the Holocaust and slavery and other instances of extermination and exploitation can serve well here. These stories can be told both as formal history lessons with mind numbing statistics (6,000,000 Jews, 500,000 Gypsies, 1,000,000 Cambodians, all slaughtered in the name of a higher morality) and in terms of particular individuals with whom students can empathize (Anne Frank, Rosa Parks, slave autobiographies), as well as by giving students models of individuals and communities that reached out beyond their own groups to help or rescue people from another group, often putting themselves and their own families in great danger. Instances of this kind of extraordinary moral heroism include the stories of Christian rescuers of Jews during the

Holocaust and Whites who helped organize the Underground Railroad to assist Blacks in escaping from slavery.

Encouraging children to appreciate other cultures doesn't mean asking them to adopt an attitude of blind cultural relativism that disallows moral judgments of practices in other cultures. We don't want our children to think that cannibalism, ritual sacrifice, head hunting, the exposure of female infants, clitoral mutilation, or even corporate bribery are morally acceptable because they are simply "the way things are done" in another culture.

Nor does an appreciation of other cultures mean the kinds of historical distortions that are sometimes promulgated under the guise of multiculturalism. Multiculturalism does a great service when it increases student awareness of, and respect for, the achievements and perspectives of women and ethnic minorities, as well as of cultures outside mainstream Western traditions. These are truths that have been waiting too long to be told.

But multiculturalism becomes divisive and inflammatory when its purpose is the denigration of core Western contributions (say, by casting aspersions on "dead, white, males"). Old distortions about Western and non-Western societies are then "corrected" by new distortions, and the focus then is not on inquiry but indictment. For instance, in teaching the American Constitution one can focus on the facts that it sanctioned slavery (until 1865) and disenfranchised women (until 1920), or on its revolutionary and liberating vision of human rights and representative government. The failures of the "founding fathers" must certainly be taught, but if the primary lesson on the Constitution is not how it transformed our conceptions of law and authority then a good deal of world history during the past 200 years will be misconceived and our students will have a hard time understanding why Thomas Jefferson and James Madison are heroes today in Warsaw, Moscow, Peking, and Soweto.

Moral zealots try to convince others to let them do their thinking for them, but our society no longer accepts "I was just following orders" as an excuse for mistreating others. Each individual is responsible for his or her own actions. But keep in mind that personal responsibility becomes a sensitive issue when directives come from religious sources. If Thomas

Jefferson (or any honored person) promotes something we consider morally repugnant (say, that slavery is acceptable), we have no problem as teachers discussing the moral implications of the position and presenting alternate viewpoints. We are not obliged to accept all of Jefferson's or anyone else's views. Indeed, we can honor Jefferson for those positions that we believe enhanced human liberty and condemn him for those that we believe did the opposite. But when the source of the position is said to be God, rejecting the position on moral grounds is problematic. One is not supposed to question God's morality (even though many of God's actions would be considered immoral if done a person).

As teachers, the best we can do is present the different sides of moral controversies as honestly as possible. The question then arises, should teachers present their own views on moral issues? On certain "settled" issues, such as slavery, the Holocaust, racism, and anti-Semitism, few of us would want teachers to take a neutral stand, simply presenting pro's and con's. And the fact that all of these repugnant positions have been propounded by major religious figures, citing scripture for support, would not convince most of us that a neutral stand is appropriate.

But what about areas of current controversy, especially those in which strong religious positions have been taken, such as abortion, stem cell research, and homosexual rights? If a school takes its responsibility as moral educator seriously, then these issues will have to be discussed. Some time will need to be set aside for thoughtful analysis of such "current events." But should teachers go beyond presenting different sides of a controversy and state their own position? We obviously don't want children to adopt the teacher's side on an issue to please (or avoid displeasing) him or her.

Each school should give thoughtful consideration to this question. My recommendation is that teachers be allowed to state their positions during discussions of moral issues and that it be made public that this is school policy. Students will be less coercible if they know that open public debate with everyone free to take sides is an inherent aspect of the educational program. If teachers take a side then they should make it very clear that this is what they are doing and they should explain the reasons behind their views, such as whether they are based on evidence or faith.

At the same time teachers should present other sides honestly and treat student positions respectfully. This may not be easy when teachers have strong feelings on an issue, and they will have to remind themselves that their role in these discussions is to foster moral reasoning, not to gain converts. Their proper role is to help students recognize and evaluate their assumptions, emotions, and intentions, the accuracy of their information, and the logic of their arguments. It is not the teacher's role to punish students, through sarcasm, rejection, impatience, derision or any other means, for their positions. Too often, students complain that they have to regurgitate their teacher's version of the PC (politically correct) position in order to get a good grade.

Religiously affiliated schools obviously educate students to believe in the tenets of their religion, as is their right. Each religion has its creation story, its heroes, and its requirements for leading a virtuous life and getting into heaven (if the religion includes the notion of heaven). But I'd suggest that schools with religious affiliations take into consideration that we are a pluralistic society, with many different religions and many people with no religion, and that, by law, no religion is allowed to dictate to any other. Some religions teach that everyone who doesn't join their ranks and believe as they believe is inherently immoral, even evil. This kind of intolerance teaches children that it is okay to judge people, not by their acts, not by their kindness and fairness, but by their beliefs. This plants in the child seeds of alienation from much of the human race. As an educational practice, aside from being of questionable morality, it doesn't prepare a child for life in our society or in the wider, global society that we all now inhabit. A better attitude to teach is captured in the famous epigram attributed to Voltaire, "I disapprove of what you say, but I will defend to the death your right to say it."

In the next chapter, we will cover the question How do children acquire morals? But first a bit more needs to be said about school administrators as sources of moral inspiration. In my work with schools, I usually ask teachers what they have done with students that they would call moral education. The reply of a middle school teacher in a suburban New Jersey community was instructive. He acknowledged that he does very little now that he would call moral education but that a few years earlier, under the leadership of a particular principal, he and other teachers were much more prone to think about the character education of their pupils.

Under this principal, who was only there for one year on a temporary appointment, morals and morale were viewed as high priority items. The teacher mentioned that on the surface the changes initiated by the principal were not that dramatic, yet his impact on interpersonal relationships was profound. "It was primarily his focus on feelings—both students' and teachers'—when any problems arose, along with his determination that everyone in the school would be treated with respect and consideration. Everyone counted."

One simple innovation involved weekly certificates acknowledging student helpfulness. The teacher said that this led him to pay attention to students that he might otherwise not have noticed. For example, he realized that one boy, who had not stood out in any particular way before, was exceptionally courteous and helpful, doing many "small" things such as complimenting another student who did something well, holding the door for other students, and pitching in readily when the room had to be prepared for special projects or cleaned up.

The principal also set a good example for dealing with rule infractions. For example, one day a nine-year-old boy brought his pet mouse to school. This youngster was a bit of a discipline problem and the teacher, who was uncomfortable with mice, said he was about to scold the boy and send him to the principal when the principal happened to walk by. The teacher informed the principal of the mouse and to his surprise the principal treated the boy in a friendly manner. He asked the boy about where he keeps the mouse and what the mouse does. He also asked the boy why he brought the mouse to school and the boy replied that the heat was off in his home and he was afraid the mouse would get sick or freeze. The boy also acknowledged that he wanted to show the mouse to his classmates. He thought kids might not be so afraid of mice and mean to them if they saw how nice they are.

The principal told the boy how moved he was by his affection for the mouse and then explained why bringing a mouse to school could cause problems by distracting students from their work. He asked the boy not to bring the mouse again unless it was an emergency and the boy agreed. Then the principal gave the boy a minute to show his mouse around and told him that during recess he could teach any of his classmates who were interested about mice and how to care for them. Then they found a box for the mouse ("He needs air holes," explained the boy) and the principal set it on a bookshelf in his office. The boy could not have been happier and more cooperative.

The teacher was impressed that what he had viewed as merely an act of rule breaking and a challenge to his authority had been transformed by the principal into an affirmative human exchange. To be sure, the principal upheld the rule and explained its purpose, but his primary aim was to let the boy know that his feelings were important, that he was a member of a caring community. The teacher also recognized that the principal, by not making it an issue about authority, enhanced his authority.

The teacher said that because of the principal's certificate program and other aspects of his leadership, he and other teachers paid more attention to, and were more openly appreciative of, students' cooperative and kind behavior than they had been before. He added that school then became a much more enriching environment for both students and teachers, not just with regard to academic excellence, but for social and emotional growth as well. The "caring community" spirit had begun to replace the sense that the teacher's job is to control the students while the students do their best to avoid being controlled.

Character education was not a formal part of the next principal's agenda and the emphasis reverted to academic and athletic achievement, competition, and maintaining discipline. The old estrangement between students and teachers quickly returned and struggles over authority and control became more frequent. School then became a less pleasant place to spend one's days.

Schools are more readily turned into caring communities when the school leadership starts from the belief that the school is a sacred place in which the torch of human civilization is passed directly from teachers into the hands of students, from person to person. From this perspective teaching is an act of love and intimacy. This is something both teachers and students need to feel. It makes the whole educational enterprise more exciting and important.

School leaders should find that it is not that difficult to inspire students and teachers, to make them feel they are part of an admirable, moral endeavor and that their individual contributions are crucial to its success. We all want to feel that.

CHAPTER 2

HOW CHILDREN DEVELOP MORALS
AND MORAL STYLES

Mark Twain said, "There are several good protections against temptations but the surest is cowardice." Surely one motivation for treating others well (or at least not doing them harm) is the fear of punishment. But just as assuredly there are other "internal" motivations—motivations based on compassion and principle. We call these moral motivations.

The three basic processes through which children develop morals—meaning, simply, the inclination to treat others kindly and fairly—are:

♦ internalizing the values of moral models (also called morality through affiliations),

♦ forming moral principles, which are personal standards of right and wrong that promote a strong sense of obligation to treat others kindly and fairly, and

♦ experiencing empathy for others.

In everyday terms, one might say we become moral because we are moved by people's feelings, moved by the goodness of moral models, and moved by ideas of the "good," such as noble principles and ideals[1].

Associated with each of these moral motivational processes are moral emotions, positive and negative feeling states that influence the kind of actions we take toward others. For example, once children internalize the standards of an adult they love and admire, violating those standards makes them feel unworthy of the adult's (the parent's, the teacher's, the coach's) love and ashamed to face him or her. Harming someone with whom one empathizes arouses guilt. And violating personal standards produces self-loathing or shame in oneself. So, children try to do what they know is right

---

1 For a detailed analysis of these processes see *Bringing Up a Moral Child* by Michael Schulman and Eva Mekler, Addison-Wesley Publishers, 1985; revised edition, Doubleday, 1994, and my chapter "How We Become Moral" in *The Handbook of Positive Psychology*, edited by C. R. Snyder and S.J. Lopez, Oxford University Press, 2002, pages 499-512.

in order to avoid feeling shame, guilt, or self-loathing.

On the positive side, when children live up to the standards they have internalized from someone they love and admire, they feel proud and worthy of that person's love. And they experience empathic joy when making someone with whom they empathize feel good. And they experience a sense of personal integrity or wholeness when living up to their own standards. So, to feel proud, joyous, and whole, they try to do what they know is right.

All the positive and negative moral emotions I've mentioned arise from a person's own actions and intentions toward others. Another set of moral emotions arises from witnessing others engaging in acts of harming or helping. For example, our empathy for friends or family members might make us angry at someone who harms them, or arouse tender feelings toward someone who helps them. Or we might experience awe in response to people who remain true to their principles despite hardships or threats (and, in contrast, be repulsed by those who abandon principles at the slightest temptation). And our pride at being a member of a righteous group might be aroused whenever another member does something noble (and, in contrast, we might feel humiliation in reaction to a member's betrayal of the group's ideals).

INTERNALIZATION

In everyday terms, the internalization of adult standards means that the child learns to say to himself the behavioral rules he has heard from the significant adults in his life, the adults he cares about and identifies with, and, therefore, wants to model himself after. Internalization is most likely to occur when a youngster is given clear and forcefully stated rules and good reasons for them. But keep in mind that children only internalize the rules of adults they love or admire. They may obey the rules of others for practical reasons (to avoid punishment or because they find the rule suits their interests), but with internalization they live up to the rules on their own because they want to feel worthy of the person they love. Internalization can be thought of as morality through affiliation.

In order for a child to internalize a teacher's standards the teacher must stand for something and make her position and her reasons clear. Teachers who adopt a neutral position on moral issues will not be effective moral educators. Here is an example of a teacher doing what I believe is an effective job of moral education with a six-year-old boy:

The boy's classmate, Brigit, had come up to the teacher, face full of smiles, to show her some drawings she had just completed. The little boy, Albert, was standing near the teacher's desk and when he saw Brigit hand over the drawings, without really looking at them he promptly remarked, "They stink."

Brigit's smile vanished. The teacher took Albert aside, bent down to him and said, "You may not know it, but that hurt Brigit's feelings because she really worked hard on those pictures. Now, I'm sure if you knew that you were going to hurt her feelings, you wouldn't have said that about them. I don't think you'd ever want to be that kind of boy, would you?"

Albert swallowed, and with his face down, he muttered, "No." His teacher then took his hand and said, "Come, let's take a good look at her pictures together, and we'll each tell her which one we like best."[2]

This teacher took a very forceful stand, although she did not simply scold or punish Albert. What she did was remind him of a standard he already understood, but that had not yet become a guiding principle for his actions. Even though she didn't state the standard formally (she used indirect, "attributional" techniques), her primary message that "It is bad to hurt people intentionally" came through very clearly.

The teacher attributed good intentions to Albert and treated him lovingly. She also provided him with a model of caring. She was taking care of Brigit's feelings and guided him to engage in caring behaviors himself. But she also let Albert know that he was jeopardizing his standing in the "good guys" club by his treatment of Brigit. Because Albert cared very much about his teacher's opinion of him (but not yet about Brigit's feelings), he was willing to behave according to her standards. By accepting her standards he would not only be doing what he knew was right (children know intuitively that harming someone is wrong), he would secure his status as a good guy. The teacher, by modeling how to treat Brigit and guiding Albert's behavior, was taking responsibility for teaching caring, not just criticizing.

Did this teacher have the right to handle Albert this way, to try to determine his sense of right and wrong? I think she did. One of the responsibilities of being an adult is to pass on to children the moral heritage of one's community. It has become almost axiomatic among educators that

---

2 From *Bringing Up a Moral Child.*

when disciplining a child, condemn the behavior but never the child. It is a good rule. On the other hand, when it comes to praising, I recommend that teachers and parents praise both the behavior and the child. It is helpful for a child to hear that his teacher thinks he has a kind heart or is a trustworthy person (only if she really believes it, of course). It will help him develop an identity as a good person. It is also useful if he knows that his actions can jeopardize that lofty status.

Teachers need to take strong stands about kindness and fairness. No teacher likes to see children being teased or ridiculed, but some consider teasing a natural and inevitable stage that children go through, and they don't handle it very forcefully. Others cannot bear to see children hurting each other and take a strong stand, communicating:

No one has the right to hurt anyone's feelings in this class. That is an absolute rule. Everybody's feelings in this room count, including mine. My job is to make sure that every child here finishes the day feeling good about himself or herself, and I need your help to do that. So there will be no teasing, no name calling, no gossiping, no leaving anyone out. We cannot have a happy class if any of that goes on.

Children respond well to this kind of forceful establishment of moral standards. They know that what the teacher stands for is good and they respect her for it. They recognize that her firmness is not motivated by some personal need to exert power over them, but that it is an act of love, to protect all of their feelings. When children feel cared about and see the adults around them as caring people, caring becomes a natural element in their world, not something unusual or burdensome.

Since internalization involves talking to oneself, teachers can facilitate this process by giving children what to say to themselves and when to say it: "The next time you are about to tease someone, I want you to tell yourself, 'No. This will hurt my classmate's feelings and ruin our class. I won't do it. If I have something to say I'll say it in a positive way.'" Teachers can even have students rehearse this in their imaginations by having them picture themselves in an exchange with someone who brings out the teaser in them.

Internalization is a process that continues through childhood and adulthood, whenever we have a beloved teacher or mentor. We carry their voices and faces with us. One of my favorite examples is attributed to Jawaharlal Nehru, the first prime minister of India, who, whenever he was confronted with a difficult political decision, would remember and try to be guided by these words of Gandhi:

> Whenever you are in doubt or when the self becomes too much with you, try the following expedient: Recall the face of the poorest and most helpless man you have ever seen and ask yourself if the step you contemplate is going to be of any use to him. Will he be able to gain anything by it? Will it restore to him control over his own life and destiny? In other words, will it lead to...self-rule for the hungry and spiritually starved millions of our countrymen? Then you will find your doubts and your self melting away.

Stories of moral heroes are powerful tools for helping children acquire and internalize standards of kindness and fairness. Children are naturally susceptible to being inspired by stories of people of honor, compassion, and moral courage. In a sense, they become inhabited by these moral exemplars, and from then on are prone to be guided by their moral messages. This is a unique human characteristic. One might say that we are the inspirable species.

DEVELOPING PERSONAL STANDARDS

While internalization is a powerful motivational force, ultimately children need to develop their own principles based on their determination of how they should conduct their lives and what kind of world they want to help create. In other words, children need ideals, visions of the best kind of person to be and the best kind of community to live in, regardless of the approval or disapproval of parents, teachers, or any other authority.

A child's commitment to treating others well grows as he comes to understand that in the long run the world becomes a better place to live in when he takes other people's interests into consideration. Personal moral standards are rules of conduct that are sustained by our imaginations because we can foresee what it would be like to live in a world in which kindness and justice prevail. The best known personal standard is "Do unto others as you would have them do unto you." When a child strives to live up to that standard, she will think carefully about how she treats others. Similarly, a child who believes in the principles "Play fair" and "It's not whether you win or lose, it's how you play the game" will compete differently than one who believes "Winning isn't everything; it's the only thing." Teachers can help young people reason their way toward principles about how they should behave in various domains in their lives, from friendships to the way they conduct themselves in the community. Here is an example of a teacher using a Socratic dialogue to help a child reason his way to a new vision of what he should demand of himself and of his "friends."

TEACHER: You say you knew it was wrong to vandalize school property, but you went along with your friends because you didn't want them to make fun of you.

CHILD: Yes, they would have called me a nerd.

TEACHER: Why was it wrong to vandalize the property?

CHILD: I know those things are expensive to replace or repair.

TEACHER: But if you didn't do it, your friends would have made fun of you?

CHILD: Yes.

TEACHER: It doesn't sound like they are really your friends.

CHILD: What do you mean?

TEACHER: Well, would a friend make fun of someone who stands up for what he thinks is right? I don't think that person is much of a friend, do you? Would you make fun of a friend because he voiced his feelings about what he thought was right?

CHILD: I don't think so.

TEACHER: I think you need to ask yourself why you've selected friends whose values you don't respect. I think you also need to ask yourself if they really are your friends. Friendship is a very special relationship, involving caring and respect. Do you think your relationship with the boys you are calling your friends involves caring and respect?

CHILD: Sometimes, not all the time.

TEACHER: Think about whether, as a friend, you have a right to receive caring and respect all the time. Actually, I don't think you were much of a friend to them. It doesn't sound like you cared much about them.

CHILD: Why?

TEACHER: Well, if you are truly someone's friend, and you know he is about to do something that you believe is genuinely wrong, really destructive, wouldn't you have a responsibility to let him know that he is headed down a destructive path? Shouldn't friends try to help each other become the best people they can be?

CHILD: I guess they should.

TEACHER: Think of someone you admire, someone you know or have read about who you think is a good person. Does someone come to mind?

CHILD: Yes.

TEACHER: Good. Close your eyes and imagine him or her in the situation that you were in with your friends. Imagine you are watching a movie of that situation with the person you admire seeing what the others are planning. Just picture what he or she would do and say.

CHILD: He'd try to stop them.

TEACHER: Would they call him names?

CHILD: He wouldn't care. Their names wouldn't hurt him and they'd see that and stop.

TEACHER: Doing the right thing often involves a risk, but frequently the risk isn't as big as we think. Kids tend to respect other kids who stand up for what is right. Doing things we know are wrong also involves risks. We walk around feeling bad about ourselves, we damage our friendships or our communities, and sometimes we fool ourselves into believing things that aren't true, such as that people care about us who really don't. Think about these things the next time you are about to do something that violates your own sense of right and wrong.

By helping students reason their way to standards of moral excellence, teachers are engaging the child's natural drive for mastery and steering it toward moral ends. In other words, they are inspiring the child to define a moral person as the best kind of person to be. At the same time, it is important to help youngsters recognize that moral action often involves risk (as the dialogue above indicates), but that not taking an action one knows to be right involves risk too, such as the risk of deluding oneself about one's friends or the risk of living one's life in a community that is unjust and oppressive.

We honor moral heroes like Gandhi and Martin Luther King, Jr., not because they were wimps who could be pushed around or because they took the easy way out and went along with the crowd, but because they have been the most steadfast and courageous among us. They took great risks to stand up for what they knew to be right. Most children are attracted to courage and want to think of themselves as courageous, but often they don't recognize the courage in moral behavior. They may ascribe more courage to the bully than to the child who intercedes for the victim with a tremulous "Leave him alone." The bully seems powerful and power is appealing to most children. Therefore it is important for teachers to help children recognize the difference between the power of those who destroy and the power of those who build and create and help.

Here again there is value in teaching about moral heroes. It helps youngsters appreciate that they will be in the best of company if they too strive to live up to moral principals, and it will help them muster their own courage when they are called upon to take risks in order to do what they know is right.

EMPATHY

The third source of moral motivation is empathy, which refers to the miraculous capacity we all have to feel other people's feelings, to imagine ourselves in their place and experience their joys and sorrows. Teachers can foster empathy by giving students reminders such as, "Think what she's feeling now," "Remember how you felt when you were treated that way?" and "Think how you'd feel if that was done to you." When simple reminders aren't sufficient, giving a child more detailed information about the other person's position—especially about his or her strivings and struggles—and then having the child imagine or role-play the other person's experiences, should have a stronger impact.

Children have a natural capacity for empathy, but it tends not to extend to people not considered "us." Not us can be the nerds, the niggers, the Jews, the freshmen, the girls, the wetbacks, the gays, the Indians, the wops, or any other group. The sociologist Robert Merton has written about the irrationality of out-group prejudice:

> The very same behavior undergoes a complete change of evaluation in its transition from the in-group...to the out-group.... Did Lincoln work far into the night? This testifies that he was industrious, resolute, perseverant, and eager to realize his capacities

to the full. Do the out-group Jews or Japanese keep these same hours? This only bears witness to their sweatshop mentality, their ruthless undercutting of American standards, their unfair competitive practices. Is the in-group hero frugal, thrifty, and sparing? Then the out-group victim is stingy, miserly, and penny-pinching.[3]

Teachers can use books, poems, and essays to break the in-group/out-group barrier and extend the boundaries of who students can empathize with. "Huckleberry Finn" and "The Diary of Anne Frank" provide powerful lessons, as does the poem Incident[4] by Countee Cullen:

> Once riding in old Baltimore,
> Heart-filled, head-filled with glee,
> I saw a Baltimorean
> Keep looking straight at me.

> Now I was eight and very small,
> And he was no whit bigger,
> And so I smiled, but he poked out
> His tongue, and called me, "Nigger."

> I saw the whole of Baltimore
> From May until December;
> Of all the things that happened there
> That's all that I remember.

Another useful lesson can be found in the words of Pastor Martin Neimoeller, a German clergyman during the Nazi era:

> In Germany they first came for the Communists, and I didn't speak up because I wasn't a Communist. Then they came for the Jews, and I didn't speak up because I wasn't a Jew. Then they came for the trade unionists, and I didn't speak up because I wasn't a trade unionist. Then they came for the Catholics, and I didn't speak up

---

3 From Robert Merton's *Social Theory and Social Structure*, The Free Press, 1957.

4 From the collection, *Colors* by Countee Cullen, published by Harper & Brothers, 1925.

because I was Protestant. Then they came for me. And by that time no one was left to speak up.[5]

One can also use the following incident in which a mother helped her son extend the boundary of who should be considered "us" and worthy of our care. She had come across a taunting letter that her teenage son and his friends were planning to send to a schoolmate whom they considered effeminate and thought was homosexual. This mother was extremely distressed that her son could be so cruel and insensitive and asked him to terminate the conspiracy. The boy resisted saying, "Oh mom, he's a faggot," as if this justified his nastiness.

His mother became very forceful with him and explained why she could not let him hurt this other boy. She reminded him that she had spent part of her youth in India when it was still an English colony. Her parents were Greek and her father was in the Greek foreign service, stationed in India, and they lived in the European compound in New Dehli. Since she was olive skinned, the other children thought she was half Caucasian and half Indian and called her "half-breed" and other nasty names and refused to play with her. She said that it was terribly painful for her and that she could not let her son inflict that kind of pain on another child simply because he is different.

The boy, who had not been able to empathize with his classmate who seemed so alien, was able to empathize with his mother and could then make the connection to the other boy's feelings. He convinced his friends to drop their scheme.

Children come into the world with inborn capacities to develop compassion and principles (both of which act as counterforces to their inborn capacities for aggressiveness and avarice) and they are very susceptible to moral instruction. Teachers will not find it that hard.

MORAL STYLES

For most children, their morality springs from all three sources of moral motivation—they feel empathy, they are guided by principles, and they have internalized standards derived from the important people and

5 Attributed to Pastor Martin Neimoeller. In E. Morison Beck (ed.), *John Bartlett's Familiar Quotations*. Boston: Little, Brown & Co., 1980, p. 824.

groups in their lives. But the relative strength of each source varies from individual to individual, and this seems to be an inborn characteristic, visible from an early age. For example, a child might not have much empathy for others in one-on-one relationships, but have a strong sense of principle (this child might be more likely to become a civil rights lawyer than a social worker). Another child's main source of morality might be his or her moral affiliations (e.g., wanting to be a good Scout). A third might have a big, empathic heart and not think much about the principles of right and wrong. In other words, each child will have his or her own moral style. The sociopath will, of course, be low on all three sources of morality.

As teachers get to know students, they will find it helpful to try to assess their dominant moral style (if they have one). That way they can tailor their moral messages more precisely. For example, for a child who is more inclined toward principle than empathy, saying "What if everyone did that" would be a more effective message than saying "Think how you'd feel if that were done to you." The former question asks him to think about the rule and what would happen if everyone broke it; the latter tries to get him to put himself in the other person's place. For another child, one with strong moral affiliations, it might be better to ask, "What if the coach knew that you acted that way?" For most children, all three types of appeals are likely to have an impact, but tapping into the child's dominant moral style offers the best chance to produce the desired moral growth.

CHAPTER 3
THE CURRICULUM

For schools to become moral communities, moral concerns must enter the curriculum in a much fuller way than usual. Moral lessons cannot be consigned to special classes that meet once or twice a week, and they cannot be thought of as something we do when we are not too busy with our course work. Indeed, moral lessons properly integrated into the curriculum should enhance learning and complement standard academic goals.

In general, the aim is to reconceive course materials to:

a) draw out the moral implications of the subject matter, and

b) highlight the personal strivings for excellence that lay behind whatever advances have been made in each field of study.

For example, history can be conceived, not merely as the playing out of economic dialectics or the product of "great" figures and great wars, but as a continuing struggle by individuals and communities to make the world a more humane and satisfying place (at least for their own people).

Interpretations of history are valued in terms of their usefulness in helping us tell a coherent story of the past, as well as for their ability to help us make sense of the present and prepare for the future. An interpretation that takes account of moral striving will, I believe, turn out to be a useful supplement to other perspectives, augmenting our understanding of the evolution of political, economic, and religious systems, as well as of cultural and artistic developments.

The laws, migrations, political rhetoric, and technological innovations of an era can certainly be analyzed in terms of both individual moral motivations and their impact on social conditions.

Contemporary historians (as well as psychologists and other social scientists) generally dismiss the importance of moral motivations. At best, they view moral motives as derived from "more basic" selfish and acquisitive or "economic" impulses. For example, traditional psychological theory interprets love and kindness, not as autonomous impulses, but as expressions of dependency or affiliative needs. Similarly, historians tend to view an ostensibly moral event like the Civil War as essentially an economic competition between the North and South over which region would dominate the nation, not at its root a conflict over slavery. Other views are dismissed as naive. But this emphasis on selfish impulses, by ignoring or minimizing the significance of moral motives, yields an incomplete understanding of human nature and human motivation. Contrary to traditional social science theory, a great deal of developmental research indicates that our moral motives—those based on empathy, love, and conscience—are as fundamental to our natures as our selfish ones. They are evident during the child's first years and remain significant throughout the lifespan. Teachers need not fear that they are conveying unsophisticated viewpoints when they include moral motivations in their interpretations of history and human events.

Mathematics can be taught, not simply as a set of operations, but as the achievement of extraordinary individual and collective efforts by people from virtually every major culture, spanning thousands of years. Many students do not find mathematics as fascinating as their teachers would like. To many, math beyond the basic arithmetic operations seems useless—a collection of arcane puzzles, of value only to those who intend to become mathematicians, scientists, or engineers.

As educators, we would have a better shot at exciting our students about math (or at least helping them appreciate it as a grand human adventure) if we taught them about the lives of mathematicians, their strivings and struggles, so they understand what mathematicians do. They need to know that Pythagoras was a person, not just a theorem, and that Newton and Leibniz invented the calculus, not to torture math students, but because there was no useful way to calculate continuously changing events (such as the changing velocity of a missile in flight).

We can also do a better job helping students appreciate the practical value of mathematical achievements, such as in space travel and astronomy, building and boat design, and many other areas of everyday life. Students need not be able to do calculus to grasp, and find interesting, some of the mathematical thinking involved in planning the trajectories of spacecraft or figuring out the stresses in grand structures like the pyramids and the George Washington Bridge. By teaching math in terms of human striving, we might even be able to give students an appreciation of mathematicians' never-ending quest to learn more about the mathematical universe, about numbers, sets, and topographies, among many other mathematical domains.

Literature can obviously be analyzed for its moral implications. Stories for youngsters are often about finding one's way through moral dilemmas, and the moral messages of many "classics" for both children and adults are quite evident. For example, the major stories of Charles Dickens, Victor Hugo, Mark Twain, and Upton Sinclair are driven by explicit moral concerns. The moral positions of some authors, like Camus, Sartre, and other existentialists, are direct reflections of their philosophical analyses of the human condition. With some authors, their moral positions are less clear (as in Shakespeare's *The Merchant of Venice*) or perhaps not there at all.

There is an important trap to be aware of here, lest we wind up with an American version of Soviet realism where art becomes, essentially, a form of propaganda. The purpose in assessing the moral implications of literature is not to leave out or downplay aesthetic issues or to judge the quality of writing in terms of its moral messages. Stories with strong moral messages can be written poorly and those with questionable morality can be written well. In a literature class one wants to pick stories and poems on the basis of their literary merit, but many great works also present richly depicted moral positions.

The goal of analyzing stories and poems in terms of their moral messages is definitely not to come up with a set of "politically correct" works. Rather, the purpose is to embed stories in their culture, to try to understand a work's impact on (and reflection of) its time, as well as its continuing impact on our time.

These are just three examples of how standard course work can introduce students to the most lofty expressions of human striving, including moral striving, while still meeting academic objectives. Virtually any course can be enhanced in this way. Moreover, students should understand that intellectual advancement is a collective endeavor, in which even the most outstanding achievements are the product of many minds searching for truth. Isaac Newton said it this way:

> If I have seen a little further it is by standing on the shoulders of Giants.

One additional point. Some teachers in civics and social studies courses emphasize only the negative aspects of our nation, such as our racial and economic inequities. Wanting to rouse their students' moral outrage, they frequently leave them merely demoralized and alienated. In these classes little is taught about the substantial improvements in race relations and economic conditions that have taken place in our country during the past fifty years. And little is said about the many men and women, black and white, in and out of government, who dedicated, risked, and sometimes gave their lives to bring about these changes. Instead, every racial incident and corporate scandal is trumpeted as confirmation of the slogan that we are, fundamentally and irrevocably, a racist and exploitative society.

Besides giving students a distorted view of American history and culture, this one-sided approach leaves them with the cynical and hopeless feeling that nothing can be done to make things better. Instead, we need to teach our students what has been done, and is now being done, to right the wrongs in our society; and we need to inspire them with the words and deeds of those who have led the struggle for racial and economic justice. We must not gloss over the problems in our society, but it is crucial that we teach our students, as earlier generations were taught, that we live in a land of possibilities, with institutions that permit us to continually renew ourselves and move closer toward our highest ideals.

Lessons on Human Nature

Our schools do not ordinarily have courses on human nature. Nevertheless, many courses do provide students with a vision of human nature, one that is, to say the least, not very flattering. In biology classes we teach about the selfish gene and that altruism is just another form of self-interest. Our social studies and history classes focus on warfare, slavery, totalitarianism, and other forms of "man's inhumanity to man." Even our lessons on great American leaders like Jefferson, Lincoln, and Roosevelt—in our desire to present a sophisticated rendering—will often stress their failings (their peccadilloes, their inability to rise totally above the prejudices of their time, their political horse trading) virtually as much as their achievements.

In social science classes we introduce students to Freud, who said that it is only fear of punishment and the constraints of civilization that keep our bestial instincts in check. Or we teach Stanley Milgram's "obedience" study in which people gave others what they believed to be strong electric shocks simply because they were told to. Our literature students read *Lord of the Flies* and *All Quiet on the Western Front*, among other stories that depict human beings at their worst. Even our religious curriculums sometimes send the same gloomy message, teaching that it is only religion that gives humans any semblance of morality.

We encourage our students to keep abreast of current events, but our news sources, too, present young people with a loathsome view of human nature. Murders are news. But on a day when there are no murders or even attempted murders, they are not likely to see a headline that reads "Everybody Got Along Pretty Well Today."

The overall message for our children is that morality does not come naturally to us, or that if it does it is easily overwhelmed by the darker forces of our nature. There is no question that we humans can be vicious, selfish, greedy, and corrupt, but we are also kind and self-sacrificing, and we love justice and fair play. And these "moral" impulses are as natural to us as our baser impulses, and actually more pervasive. The evidence is all around us and a curriculum that leaves out human goodness is a distortion of the truth.

In truth, most of us do get along pretty well every day. We consider murder and thievery aberrations, not the norm, and even in the most crime-ridden neighborhoods, most people do not commit crimes. As I've mentioned , children as young as two, before much "civilizing" or religious training has occurred, spontaneously exhibit empathy for others, and many try to comfort others who are hurt. And by three or four, many display a sense of right and wrong, understanding that harming is bad and helping is good. Indeed, morality is so much a part of our nature, and clearly so crucial for our survival as a species, that (as described in the last chapter) it has evolved in three independent forms, one based on empathy, one based on principles of right and wrong, and one based on wanting to live up to the standards of the good people we love.

Why do young children love television shows like *Barney* and *Mr. Rogers*—programs with neither adventure nor exciting special effects? It is because these characters exemplify goodness and children are naturally attracted to goodness (it is also why we adults return to *It's a Wonderful Life* every Christmas). To mention one of many studies that could be cited, researchers observed 26 three- to five-year-old children during 30 hours of free play in a preschool. During that time, they recorded approximately 1,200 "altruistic" acts, including sharing, cooperating, helping, and comforting.[6] It is in our nature to share, cooperate, help, and comfort, which is why people jump into frozen lakes to rescue strangers and risk their lives to fight injustice against people they have never even met (as just one example, recall Andrew Goodman, Michael Schwerner, and James Earl Chaney, the young men who were murdered in 1964 in Mississippi while trying to register black voters).

In school we learn about many great developments that changed the course of history, like the invention of the wheel, the forging of metals into stronger and stronger weapons, and the invention of explosives and the steam engine and electronics. Here is one we don't teach: "The Golden Rule." We are all familiar with it (Do unto others as you would have them do unto you), but perhaps not how widespread it is. It is found in Christianity, Judaism, Hinduism, Confucianism, Buddhism, Taoism, and Zoroastrianism. Its universality attests to its compatibility with our nature and its impact on human behavior and society deserves much more recognition than it has received.

The renowned primatologist, Frans de Waal, makes the case for the naturalness of human morality by describing humanlike morality in chimpanzees, our closest animal relatives. In his book, *Our Inner Ape*,[7] he tells the story of Kuni, a bonobo (a kind of chimp, which is a kind of ape), who saved a starling that flew into the glass of her enclosure. She picked up the stunned bird and gently set it on its feet. When it failed to move, she tried throwing it a little but it just fluttered. She picked it up again, then climbed to the top of the tallest tree where she carefully unfolded and spread its wings. Then, "like a little toy airplane," she sent the bird out toward the edge of the enclosure.

When the bird didn't make it all the way out, Kuni climbed down and <u>stood watch over</u> it for a long time, keeping other bonobos away until it

6 F. F. Strayer, S. Wareing, and J. P. Rushton, The Social Constraints on Naturally Occurring Preschool Altruism, *Ethology and Sociobiology*, 1979, 1, 3-11.

7 Frans de Waal. *Our Inner Ape: A Leading Primatologist Explains Why We Are Who We Are*. New York: Riverhead Press, 2005.

recovered and flew off safely. De Waal wants us to appreciate that Kuni's response was not "hardwired." "She tailored her assistance to the specific situation of an animal totally different from herself."

In another of de Waal's examples, he and his colleagues had arranged for Kuif, a female chimp, to "adopt" a newborn chimp named Roosje. For a few weeks, they kept the foster mom and baby separate from the other chimps in the colony. When it was time for them to rejoin the group, de Waal feared that, Nikkie, a very aggressive, dominant male might try to kill the infant (chimps sometimes kill newborns that are not their own). He decided to introduce Kuif and Roosje to the group without Nikkie present, hoping that the other animals would embrace the mother and child and become their protectors. That's exactly what happened.

After an hour, Nikkie was finally allowed to make his entrance and, as feared, he approached Kuif and Roosje "in a most intimidating manner" with all his hair up. All eyes, human and chimp, were on him. At that moment, the two oldest males in the colony stepped in front of Nikkie, draped their arms around each other's shoulders, and stared him down. It was as if they were communicating, "You can beat one of us but not two of us, so don't even think about hurting that baby." Nikkie backed off, and when he later approached Kuif and Roosje, "under the watchful eyes of the other two males…he was nothing but gentle."

These apes, like us, can be very nasty. They can also be very kind, and their kindness, obviously, does not depend on "civilization," religion, or formal education. Kindness is in their nature—as it is in ours. And we need to make sure our students know this side of the human story.

CHAPTER 4
MORAL INQUIRY: A NEW COURSE

I highly recommend the addition to the curriculum of special course called Moral Inquiry. Such a course, drawing from psychology, sociology, philosophy, and other fields, would cover whatever is known about the forces that determine human character, particularly what influences children to grow into kind and fair people, or the opposite.

It is important that students understand that the adults in the community consider the study of moral development—how it happens, how to foster it—just as important as any other field they are asked to study, as important as mathematics, physics, literature, or art.

As in the study of any field, students need to learn about different theoretical points of view and the evidence for and against each. Also, students need to understand that, as in any area if inquiry, moral inquiry is an ongoing quest with much to be discovered.

Many topics can be covered and they can be presented at different levels of sophistication depending on the age of students. Among the topics are empathy, friendship, ideals, cooperation and competition, anger and aggression, moral reasoning, moral persuasion, altruism, guilt and shame, personal responsibility, self-discipline, parental, peer, and community influences, sex differences, sexual morality, justice, religious influences, developmental effects, rules and laws, the effects of reward and punishment, role models, love and hate, human rights, and animal rights (see my book, *Bringing Up a Moral Child*, for a framework that encompasses these and other topics).

Different aspects of topics can be presented to children at different ages. For example, young children can learn about the basic meaning of the term friendship, the different kinds of friendships, and the expectations and obligations of each. Older children can learn about the developmental stages of friendships and the characteristics that lead to one's selection or rejection as a friend. Still older children can study the moral dilemmas that derive from friendships, such as conflicts over divided loyalties, jealousies, and mismatched intimacy needs.

It should be mentioned that there are some "hot" topics pertaining to morality that have stirred up considerable intellectual and political controversy. For instance, some theorists argue that there are gender differences in morality (the early psychoanalysts thought men were inherently more moral than women; some contemporary feminists claim that women are inherently more moral than men). Other theorists assert that there are inherent racial differences in morality.

My own view, based on reading the arguments and evidence, is that there is no justification for claiming that any gender or race is morally superior to any other. For instance, while males appear to be more prone toward physical violence than women, males are just as capable of being empathic, caring, and sensitive to others. Conversely, women can be as selfish and unkind as men, and are more likely to engage in "relational aggression" using tactics like ostracism and gossip to hurt each other emotionally.

And while Blacks commit more street crimes than Whites, Whites commit more white-collar crimes.[8] Arguments for the moral superiority of one racial group over another ignore the terrible record of all races in the areas of crime, warfare, torture, genocide, and human rights abuses.

Claiming the moral high ground for one's own group may serve one's politics or one's vanity, but it cannot in any way serve the communities in which we all must find a way to live harmoniously.

---

8 For a fuller discussion of this issue, see my chapter, "The Prevention of Antisocial Behavior Through Moral Motivation Training (or *Why Isn't There More Street Crime?*)" in the book, *Protecting the Children: Strategies for Optimizing Emotional and Behavioral Development*, edited by Raymond Lorion, published by Haworth Press, 1990.

CHAPTER 5
SERVICE LEARNING

Students need to do good, not just learn to think about the good. Service projects in the school and the community, from peer tutoring to helping the elderly, can convey to students the important lesson that they too are responsible for contributing to the quality of life in their communities.

For clarity, let me distinguish service learning from two terms with which it sometimes gets confused, "work service" and "community service." Work service, when used in schools, usually refers to programs where students perform tasks beneficial to the school, as part of a school requirement, like working in the cafeteria or helping on the school grounds. Community service involves students in projects outside the school, usually with the goal of helping students understand the greater communities around them, as well as learning more about themselves in the process. Habitat for Humanity is a good example of a meaningful community service project. When schools use the term "service learning," it is usually because students are asked to engage in conscious reflection on the service they are providing. If students working with Habitat for Humanity spend time back at school studying and discussing issues related to poverty, and how Habitat for Humanity helps remedy the situation, then a good community service project also becomes a service learning project.

Many schools attempt to hook their service learning projects into specific curricular offerings, such that academic learning "informs" the service, and the service projects help students understand more deeply what they are studying. Examples might include Spanish language students volunteering in a Latino day care center, where they both practice their language skills and provide needed services, or U.S. History students working with Viet Nam veterans and learning of their personal experiences in this pivotal 20th century event. In both cases, the service and its lessons would be discussed in the classroom back at school.

Children need to understand the effort required to make things better, as well as the satisfaction that comes from making that effort. They also need to work with adults who are constructive role models and experience first hand the difference between merely complaining about the things that are wrong in the world and taking steps to make improvements.

Young people should be given as much freedom as possible to select from the range of helping activities available. It is especially important that they be made aware of the goals of their project and the obstacles to be overcome. Moreover, their ideas for solving problems should be solicited and handled respectfully. It is also worth keeping in mind that most students have little "work" experience and many will need patient guidance in order to become reliable and responsible workers. They may also need explicit instruction in how to give care and comfort, how to deal with their own frustration over not being able to turn problems around instantly, and how to remain spirited when faced with what seem like senseless bureaucratic obstacles.

In some service projects youngsters will face unhappy realities of the human condition, often for the first time in their lives. For example, in a senior citizens' center they will encounter various levels of infirmity and deterioration. They will also encounter courage, wit, and wisdom and people with an abiding passion for life, but the youngsters may be too upset, frightened, or repulsed to notice.

Project leaders will have to prepare students for what they will encounter in their work, their possible reactions, and how they are expected to behave. In an interview, Mother Teresa said that one of the criteria for selecting young women for her order is that they have "the gift of joy." Feeling sorry for people in need is not enough, she said. Indeed, communicating one's pity may make them feel ashamed. Bringing joy into their lives is the goal and this requires valuing the people one is assisting as they are right now— not treating them as a diminished version of what they were or might have been. They must see your joy in being with them.

Project leaders can help students develop the perspectives they need to fulfill their duties. For instance, they might remind those working with the elderly that we appreciate infants for what they are, and don't pity them for being inferior versions of what they are to become. Similarly, students working with the elderly can be encouraged to see the people they work with as full-fledged beings, different from what they were, but worthy and interesting as they are.

Service projects can take place within the school, such as peer tutoring, or assisting younger or disabled students in some way (coaching, tutoring, escorting, etc), or improving the physical environment (e.g., building a sandbox for kindergartners).

Projects can also take place out in the community (of course, taking into consideration student age and safety). The service project adviser might begin by making a list of the charities and service institutions in the community and noting the many different kinds of problems they address, including hunger (on a local, national, and international level), hopelessness, assisting the disabled and elderly, environmental and conservation concerns, helping disaster victims, child care, political oppression (such as Amnesty International's "Prisoners of Conscience"), voter registration, animal care, and literacy, among others.

Student projects may be able to be integrated into these organizations (some have youth coordinators), or students and advisers might come up with their own programs for making a contribution.

One goal of service projects is to teach students that there are people working day in and day out to make the world a better place, and they are having successes. Individuals can make a difference, on their own or collectively. To provide students with role models of people who are making a difference, schools might contact the Giraffe Project in Langley, Washington. The Giraffe Project honors people who have stuck their necks out to make the world a better place, and then publicizes their achievements to inspire the rest of us (a variety of educational materials are available at the Project's web site: giraffe.org). The daily news will frequently contain stories about similar people, and their stories should be brought to the attention of students. Some of these people could be invited to speak to students.

As adults, many of us do our "good works" as volunteers in various kinds of charitable and service organizations, such as hospitals, church groups, and lodges. The organization envelops us in a community of caring that provides direction and support for our altruistic inclinations, and rouses us to give of ourselves more fully than we might if we were operating strictly on our own. Unfortunately, our communities offer youngsters few such altruistic outlets. Service programs in the schools can help fill this gap, providing young people with the kinds of social supports that will bring out their best selves.

CHAPTER 6
RULES AND DISCIPLINE

If the rules in a school community (or any other community) are good rules, then they serve to better the lives of the members of the community. Therefore, we need to make sure our students understand how the rules we ask them to live by enhance their lives. Even further, we need to make sure that they believe that our purpose in imposing these rules on them is to enhance their lives. In other words, if we want our students to buy into our message about being kind and fair, we must make sure that they conclude that we are doing our best to be kind and fair to them, even when we impose rules. Ultimately, we want the children we teach to choose to be cooperative (which, turns out to be a practical as well as a moral goal since school children nowadays, unlike in earlier eras, are not easily cowed into obedience).

Therefore, in establishing rules, we need to ask four key questions:

1) Is the rule necessary for the safety and security of the children and others in the school community?

2) Is the rule necessary for effective instruction and learning?

3) Does the rule contribute to the moral atmosphere, so that students and all others in the community feel cared about, respected, and appreciated?

4) Is there a less intrusive way to accomplish the same goal so that school is more enjoyable and less restrictive?

School rules that don't meet these criteria are experienced by students as oppressive and unfair, and work against the creation of a moral community. Moreover, if the rules are to be effective guides for student behavior, it is important to frame them in terms of what to do, as well as what not to do—not merely, "We don't tease," but also, "We try to help our classmates feel good about themselves." It is also beneficial for students to understand the guiding principles behind the rules, such as, "Everyone counts here, and everyone counts equally."

Schools have many kinds of rules. Some are established at the state and school district level, covering all schools under their jurisdiction (e.g., All students must take three years of math. All schools must have fire-drills). Some rules are instituted by the school principal or other administrators and pertain only to one school (e.g., Line up when the whistle blows. You need a pass to go to the bathroom). Teachers also establish rules in their own classrooms (Raise your hand and wait to be called on. If you misbehave, you must go to the "time-out" chair). Our children are expected to learn all these rules and obey them.

School rules, like those in any ongoing institution, take on a life of their own. They are not reformulated with each new semester but continue from year to year. Ordinarily, the necessity, fairness, or practicality of a rule gets reevaluated only when some problem arises over it (such as, when students lodge a protest: "Why do the upper graders always get first choice over equipment in the gym?").

It would be impractical to have to evaluate and reestablish the entire set of school rules at the beginning of each year. Still, if we want students to feel committed to the rules, and if we want to prepare them for life in a democracy, we need to make sure they understand both the substance and purpose of the rules we ask them to follow. For schools to be safe, educational, and moral environments, everyone must accept the fairness and propriety of the rules, or at least accept that they were enacted in a fair and legitimate way.

It is helpful for teachers to go over and evaluate basic rules and policies with students, covering basic classroom requirements ("Raise your hand when you want to contribute"), safety issues ("No vanishing"), and the attitudes teachers hope to foster ("We don't laugh at mistakes; we use mistakes to learn from"). After describing each rule, it should then be examined, explaining why it was enacted and why the school feels it is a good rule. To encourage student commitment to the rule, discussion should allow students to voice objections they may have to the rule. Sometimes their objections will make sense and the rule might be in need of modification.

As an example of a way one school introduced rules, at the beginning of the academic year, every home room class went over what the school considered its "fundamental" rules. Students were given an exercise sheet that began with the statement: "Here are four types of positive behavior that are expected from all students in the school: Respectful, Cooperative, Safe, On Task. List specific actions that are examples of these four behaviors."

Next they were asked to list the opposites of the four positive behaviors, the "not allowed" behaviors, and specific actions that are examples of these negative behaviors. In the next step they had students discuss why the positive behaviors were desirable in a school and why the negative behaviors were undesirable, covering student motives for engaging in either kind of behavior. Students were then requested to give examples of their own positive and negative school behaviors, as well as why they did them (any self-revelations were voluntary). Lastly, they were asked "What can the school do to encourage more positive and less negative behaviors?"

It should be helpful if children understand that rules are a natural component of all social groups and are not just invented by the school to place restrictions on them. The Moral Inquiry class should cover the general topic of how groups make rules, including formal rules (laws, parliamentary procedures), informal rules (give an old person a seat on the bus), and unconscious rules (how far away from others we stand when we speak to them, which varies across cultures). Lessons should also cover the procedures groups have devised to change rules. Special attention should be paid to how school rules are made and how they can be changed.

It is also worth distinguishing moral rules from conventional rules from academic rules. Moral rules are about how we treat each other, about whether we are harmful or helpful, or fair or not. These are essential for making the school a good place. Conventional school rules are about establishing orderly procedures, such as which staircases to use and what clothes are appropriate. They are important rules but should be open for discussion and negotiation. Academic rules, such as completing assignments on time and using standard forms of citation in term papers, are about what the school believes students need to know and how they will do their best learning. Sometimes individual students who are capable and creative don't fit easily into the mold that the school has established for all students. Schools should consider in what ways they can be flexible to accommodate their students' individual learning styles and personalities.

One hopes that after schools educate students about school rules, they will come away with the understanding that these rules exist for the sole purpose of providing them an excellent education in a safe, sensitive, and congenial environment.

Students who live up to the rules of the community, who contribute to a safe, educational, and moral atmosphere, should be acknowledged and lauded as good citizens. This can take various forms, including personal acknowledgements by teachers and the principal, "honor" assignments (such as positions on planning committees), and "citizenship" awards.

Among the consequences schools can use when students break rules are "time out" periods (better called "time to think" periods) in areas that are set aside for contemplation; chore assignments, particularly when the chore is designed to undo the misdeed (such as scrubbing graffiti off a wall); and notification of parents, especially when a child remains emotionally detached from teachers. But any such consequence should always be accompanied by an explanation of the impact of the infraction on the people in the school community.

For example, a school principal caught some boys jamming up the urinals in the boys' bathroom. I recommended that her reprimands stress not just that a rule was broken and that money must be wasted for repairs, but also what having to deal with broken urinals and with children who act as if they hate the school does to her day. It is also beneficial for such students to consider the custodian who has to fix the urinals, and the terrible inconvenience to the students who cannot use them. She needed to explain with force and feeling that she tries to make her day about helping children learn and feel good about themselves, and that she cannot meet those goals when she must spend her time dealing with vandalism.

To make this point the principal might say something like:

> I spend all my time trying to make this a good school, one that children enjoy coming to, while you are thinking up ways to make it an unpleasant place. That tells me you aren't really reasoning about what you are doing—or that you hate this school and want to harm it. If you really don't want to harm us and it's just that you're not reasoning about what you are doing, then it's time you became more thoughtful about the impact of your behavior and started figuring out how you too can make this a better place. If you do hate the school then I need to know that, so I can try to make it a better place for you, a place you'll want to help build, not destroy.

Statements such as this, which focus on feelings and the relationship of the student to others in the community, are more likely to have a beneficial impact than merely scolding and meting out consequences.

HARASSMENT

An emphasis on feelings is also desirable when students engage in racist, sexist, or other kinds of defamatory or harassing behavior toward other students. The school's disciplinary response must be firm and swift, so that perpetrators understand that such behavior will not be allowed. But an effort should also be made to help perpetrators empathize with the target of their actions. Many schools are addressing sexual harassment with lessons in what is and isn't sexual harassment and by instituting and enforcing behavioral codes (and if warranted, contacting parents or even the police).

In the past, when girls complained of harassment by boys, schools often did little or nothing, sending girls the message that the adults in the community will not protect them, and boys the message that mistreating girls is okay. Schools are taking this issue more seriously, in part, because some parents of girls who have suffered daily taunts, gropes, and worse have sued the schools or notified the police and had the boys arrested. But it shouldn't have required lawsuits or the police for schools to address this issue.

BULLYING AND COERCION

Bullying is one of the most difficult problems that schools face, and it occurs in all kinds of schools, from inner city public schools to the most elite private schools. School is a terrible place for the victims of bullies. They get beat up, their belonging are taken from them, they are ridiculed and forced to do humiliating things. Some students simply stop going, and often won't tell anyone why out of fear or embarrassment.

One hopes that the kind of caring atmosphere advocated in this book will reduce the frequency of bullying, but, realistically, virtually all schools will have some incidents of bullying. Schools reduce bullying by being vigilant and coming down quickly and firmly on the bully. The bully needs to see the passion that administrators and teachers feel about anyone in their school being victimized. Adults need to communicate that, while they will work with the bully so that his or her best self can emerge in the school, they will take whatever steps are necessary to make sure bullying does not continue. All of the fundamental moral education tactics should be used with the bully—to arouse empathy, to engage principles, to tap into moral affiliations—but the bully also has to be absolutely certain of the "bottom line": he or she will not be allowed to harm anyone in the school.

There are different kinds of bullies, requiring different kinds of interventions. One kind is an isolated and unpopular youngster, with poor social skills, who is angry because he feels no one likes him. It can be helpful to try to find ways to integrate this type of bully into social groups in the school. Another type of bully has good social skills and is popular with other students, and may even be a clique leader. He harms others as a way of maintaining control over his entourage, essentially communicating to them, "I can be fun, but don't cross me because I can be dangerous." Because this kind of bully thrives on peer attention, it can be helpful to isolate or separate him from his crowd. His fear of being disgraced in front of his group can be used to advantage.

Other kinds of bullies include those who target classmates of a different race or ethnic group, "instrumental" bullies who menace others to get their money or other belongings, and bullies who appear to be pathological because they seem truly to enjoy hurting others. The better the teachers and administrators understand the bully's motives, the better the chance they will come up with an effective intervention strategy.

Despite a school's best efforts to create an inclusive, moral community that nurtures all students, there will be some who remain out of reach and who pose a danger to others. These "at risk" youngsters will require close supervision and counseling, and sometimes removal to a restricted educational environment where they can receive more individualized attention and cannot disrupt regular classes or pose a threat to other students or teachers.

Schools will need to establish procedures for designating that a child is "at risk" and for determining the kind of restrictions, monitoring, and counseling that are appropriate, and what the student must do to resume his or her normal status in the school. Because of intense concern about youth violence, more and more schools are adopting "zero tolerance" policies for violence, weapons possession, and other serious infractions, by suspending or expelling dangerous students, or reassigning them to special schools for similar offenders.

But some school systems make it very difficult to remove a child from a school and insist that the school find a way to work with him or her. Then administrators and teachers are faced with a difficult challenge, especially if the student refuses to be bound by any restrictions imposed and won't participate in counseling. Another challenge occurs when a misbehaving youngster's parents are not cooperative. Sometimes parents raise objections to their child being "singled out" for special placement or what they consider undue restrictions or monitoring, and some will even threaten lawsuits to prevent anything negative from going in their child's permanent record. Schools will need to prepare a policy to meet such reactions.

In general, for a school to become a moral community, certain inviolable rules have to be established. Here is one way a principal might express this:

You probably won't like every student you meet in this school, but I hope you will care about each one's feelings. But even if you don't care about someone's feelings, it is a requirement that you treat him or her as if you did. There will be fellow students who you won't want as a close friend, but it is a requirement that you be respectful to everyone and not try to make anyone feel bad.

Chapter 7
Student Participation in School Governance

Our schools are not democratic institutions. Students do not vote for principals or teachers; nor do most schools determine policies by referenda; nor do students attend voluntarily. Administrators, faculty, and students do not have the same roles or responsibilities, yet for a school to function harmoniously the members of each and every stratum must feel that their views and goals are appreciated and respected. That is the only way for administrators, faculty, and students to feel that they are all on the same side, and not (as is too common) three enemy camps locked in perpetual battle.

We want our students to become good decision makers but too often we don't give them any practice in making significant decisions. A school might even have a course in decision making skills yet not allow students the opportunity to exercise those skills in the school itself. Who should decide what students eat for lunch? When the school classrooms and hallways are scheduled to be repainted, who should select the colors? If a student breaks school rules, who should decide the consequences? And who should participate in establishing the rules in the first place?

To answer these questions, schools might learn a lesson from a recent trend in business management. Business enterprises (which ordinarily are also not democratic organizations) have been able to increase worker morale, commitment, productivity, and creativity, by instituting "participation management" governance procedures, meaning that workers at every level are given greater control over their assignments, including the policies and conditions that affect them in the workplace.

In other words, workers are given more respect and trust, and when profit sharing is included in the new arrangements, any worker effort or ingenuity that adds to company earnings increases worker salaries as well. Participation management has generally proven to be an effective and humane way to boost worker satisfaction and company profits at the same time—and similar procedures can also be of benefit in schools.

Let's take the question of what to serve for lunch. This is a common source of student complaints. They often feel that someone (the principal? the nutritionist? the cook? the Board?) is making bad decisions that affect them directly on a daily basis, and they sometimes get even by turning the lunchroom into a scene from *Animal House*. From a participation management perspective, school lunches would be an ideal area in which to give students decision making power. For instance, students could form a lunchroom committee (with faculty or administrative advisers), commissioned to improve the school lunch—and perhaps the physical atmosphere of the lunchroom as well.

Now, obviously, student decisions would have to be constrained by budgetary, nutritional, and other practical requirements. For example, students could not decide on lunches of French fries and doughnuts, nor on daily servings of filet mignon. But within reasonable constraints, which students are likely to understand and accept, the benefits of students participating in planning their own menus far outweigh any drawbacks. Not only are they likely to get better meals as a result, but they'll learn useful information about nutrition, budgets, and cooking, among other practical lessons. In addition, they'll get much needed practice in democratic decision making as they try, as a committee, to meet the challenge of creating tasty, affordable, nutritious, and varied menus for their classmates.

Will this take time? Of course, just as every other educational activity takes time, but it will be time well spent, boosting student knowledge, maturity, and morale.

ACADEMIC CHOICES

What about in academic areas? Should students have a say in what they learn or how they are taught? Here too, I believe, there are benefits from soliciting student input. The more students are involved in designing their own education, the more committed to education they will be. Again, students must work within constraints, such as state educational requirements and the school's commitment to providing the best education possible. Students will ordinarily not have sufficient knowledge to make informed judgments about course content; they can't be expected to know what they need to learn to prepare for the academic and "real" worlds they will encounter. For example, a student could not make an informed judgment about whether algebra should remain in the curriculum or which novels should be assigned. Yet there are areas in which student participation could be useful.

For example, room should be made in the curriculum for students to propose subjects for study which, if they generate sufficient interest from other students, are added as optional courses. Or, if faculty time permits, they could be taught as individual tutorials. It is not difficult to see the benefits of getting students to think about what they'd like to know and then having them participate in figuring out a way to learn it.

Sensitive faculty advisement could help students formulate or clarify what they want to know. For instance, a student who is interested in music might, with some guidance, realize that he would like to understand the differences between rock-and-roll and more traditional musical forms. A student with a new baby brother or sister might be interested in learning about infant development.

Student participation might also be useful for improving standard courses. For example, an advisory panel comprised of students who have completed a particularly troublesome course might work on ways to make the material more accessible. Administration and faculty acknowledgement that a course needs improving and that students might have some good ideas for redesigning it, should go a long way toward establishing mutually respectful and trusting relationships between students, faculty, and administrators. It seems obvious that students on the panel will learn a great deal along the way, both about the course content and about the problems teachers face in trying to make a course an enriching experience for students.

For example, while faculty will, of course, select textbooks, students have a special relationship to textbooks that teachers can tap to make their instruction more effective. To illustrate, my daughter once asked me to help her with a chapter she was having trouble with in a high school science class. I read the chapter and encountered five places that stopped me, places where I couldn't tell what the author was talking about (more specifically, how he got from the previous point to the present point he was making). With a lot of effort and rereading, I finally figured each out, but it shouldn't have been that hard. I asked my daughter to read the chapter again and show me which parts gave her trouble. She pointed out the same five spots.

The textbook author and the publisher might not have done their homework well enough by vetting the book on an appropriate student sample. But a committee of bright students with proper teacher guidance could reveal those trouble spots (which, in many cases, torment each new crop of students, year after year). The teacher could then spend more class time on those sections, or perhaps look for a better text if too many such spots are uncovered.

School Rules and Consequences

It would also be of value to have students participate in making school rules and determining consequences for violations. In any organization, when one has participated in making up the rules one has a firmer commitment to following them. This is true in small families as well as in great nations; it is also true in schools. Here's an example of student commitment from a "community meeting" in a subdivision of an inner-city high school that was attempting to implement aspects of Lawrence Kohlberg's "Just Community" approach to school governance.

At the beginning of the meeting the head of school announced that the bus for the upcoming trip to Washington might not contain enough seats for everyone who had signed up to go and that he had determined that priority would be given to students who had volunteered to help on last week's cake sale fund raiser. Student reaction was favorable. It seemed to be a fair decision although a faculty member and a few students grumbled about it having been made without first discussing it with the community.

Then a young woman, a sophomore, raised her hand and voiced an objection. She said she had helped on the cake sale and was signed up to go to Washington so, in one sense, she would benefit from the new arrangement. Yet she felt the head's decision would undermine a central tenet of their program—that students contribute their time and energy to the school because it is their school and they are trying to build a good place for learning. That framework was important to her, she continued, and explained that she felt good when she worked hard for the sake of the school. But now she was concerned that, given the decision about the bus, her future good feelings would be negated by competitive thoughts about how her actions might gain her more material rewards than her classmates.

She added that she thought it was definitely not fair to set up a connection after the fact between working for the cake sale and going to

Washington. She felt that whenever it becomes necessary for students to compete for something, everyone should know about it in advance.

Her arguments were persuasive. Other students supported her request for a vote on the head of school's decision. A vote was taken and the decision was overturned. I found this an extraordinary event to observe and a far cry from anything I ever experienced during my student days. And I came away with great respect for the head of school for encouraging this kind of student participation and allowing the democratic process to prevail. It was clear that his pride derived from witnessing the flourishing of his students' hearts and minds, and not in his ability to wield immediate power over them. If one measures his power in terms of his ability to get his students to think and to care, then his power over them was actually substantial.

There are various formats for increasing student participation in school governance. These include:

STUDENT ADVISORY COMMITTEES. These are committees in which students work with faculty members and administrators on everything from broad educational policies (such as, What are the best ways to test student learning? What should the consequences of cheating be?) to "campus life" issues (such as, What color should the walls be repainted?). Many schools already have student governments, but few student leaders feel that they have any say over central issues in their education. Too often they are restricted to decisions over such matters as the theme of the school dance and the location of the class picnic. Student contributions to school governance are too valuable to be limited to extracurricular and recreation activities.

HONOR COUNCILS. These committees, which are sometimes called "fairness committees," involve students in conflict resolution and disciplinary decisions. Any member of the school community can bring a charge to the committee that he or she was treated unfairly by another member of the community. Committees could be set up so that if the complaint is between two or more students, it would have only student members (with a faculty adviser). When a faculty member or other adult staff and a student are involved in a complaint, the committee would consist of both adult members and students. Committee members would be responsible for determining whether the claim is justified and for setting up consequences when appropriate, but their primary responsibility would be to try to improve the relationship of the parties involved. Fairness Committees can go a long way toward decreasing teasing, bullying, and tattling.

Fairness committees can also set up special mediation councils to help students in conflict work out their differences in constructive ways. It is not uncommon for students, upon seeing a conflict starting, to take sides and goad the participants into escalating their dispute into a full-blown physical confrontation. Mediation councils can provide students with a legitimate and face-saving alternative.

Community Meetings. These give students the opportunity to discuss and vote on school policies. The size of the "community" should vary with the issue under discussion and may consist of one class or all the classes from one grade or all art students or the entire school (if it isn't too large for a meaningful New England style, face-to-face town meeting).

An interesting topic to explore with students in community meetings is a student Bill of Rights, inducing students to define for themselves what they believe constitutes fair treatment in a school. It is a good forum for teaching students that with rights come responsibilities and that their rights can only be honored if they recognize and respect the rights of others in the school community, including teachers. For example, students will usually say that they want teachers to greet them cordially, that they feel they have a right to cordial treatment. Once they state that openly, they will be more likely to appreciate that teachers want, and have just as much of a right to, the very same treatment from them.

Among the rights that students may claim are the rights not to be ridiculed, to ask questions, to be encouraged, and to have the demands placed on them suit their psychological and biological "natures." One might question whether it suits children's natures to ask them to sit in silence, listening to teachers for six or more hours, day after day, month after month, year after year.

When students, like anyone else, feel that their interests have been disregarded, they become alienated and surly, and sometimes seek redress. A recent *New York Times* article (September 21, 2005) described students at DeWitt Clinton High School, an inner city school in The Bronx, engaging in a peaceful "strike" and march to protest the placement of metal detectors at entrances and a "lock down" policy that disallowed students from leaving the building during lunch. The article said the school administrators were taking the students' concerns seriously and were setting up negotiations.

This section has covered decision making in both academic and nonacademic domains and my recommendation is that administrators and teachers make a spirited effort to include students in virtually every aspect of school decision making. Moreover, the power structure of the school should itself be an area of open discussion and continuous reevaluation to find ways to render decision making more representative of the views of the entire school community and, in particular, to broaden student participation.

In other words, administrators and teachers should invite students to share power with them (and not yield it begrudgingly). Student participation in major school decisions will, I believe, function like a self-fulfilling prophesy. When students are treated as intelligent beings, worthy of respect and trust, they will rise to that level. The reverse is also true.

Open discussions about the distribution of power in the school are very important because, in truth, students are not the only ones who feel powerless. In many schools, everyone feels powerless. Students claim they have no say in any rules or procedures affecting them. Teachers feel hemmed in by bureaucratic requirements handed down from above and by unruly and unprepared students that they can't control. Principals in public schools say they can't do anything innovative because of the Superintendent's political concerns and the limitations imposed by the union contracts covering teachers and staff. Superintendents feel mired in School Board and community politics and often sense that teachers and other school personnel regard them as outsiders (and, to boot, they often have little job security). School Board members typically feel that their views get watered down in compromises with other Board members and that they are too many steps removed from the actual implementation of policies and programs to have any real control over them. Similar difficulties arise in private schools, with Boards, parent bodies, school administrators and teachers.

Schools are, indeed, complex bureaucracies, and, as is common in bureaucracies, when something goes wrong, everyone insists that it is somebody else's fault. Open discussion of the school's power structure and everyone's feelings of powerlessness can begin to shift concerns away from protecting oneself from blame to how best to bring all parties together to solve school problems and create an exceptional and humane learning environment. I have heard many stories from teachers about suffering under cruel and autocratic principals. Obviously, for a school to become a moral community, attention will have to be paid to decision making and grievance procedures at all levels.

While student participation in school decisions is to be encouraged, ultimate responsibility and authority must remain with the school administrators. It is they who must fashion and shape the academic and moral atmosphere of the school, and it is they who are ultimately accountable to boards or other governing bodies of the school.

This issue of ultimate authority (or where the "buck stops") may come up in certain extracurricular activities, such as deciding how much freedom students should have in inviting outside speakers and entertainers to the school, or whether student editors should have final say over the editorial and advertising content in the school newspaper. In recent years, administrators have been criticized for allowing student groups to invite racist or anti-semitic speakers or entertainers to the school, and for allowing student editors to accept defamatory newspaper ads (such as ads that deny the Holocaust). Such incidents are most common at the university level but they also arise in secondary schools.

The debate is often inaccurately characterized as being about free speech versus censorship. While our Constitution disallows government suppression of speech, it does not guarantee speakers or writers the right to air their views in any forum or institution they choose. We all have the right to publish our own newspaper, but we don't have the right to insist that our views be published in someone else's newspaper. On the other hand, students' and speakers' rights would definitely be violated if schools attempted to prohibit students from going to hear a particular speaker, or to punish students for reading any particular writing.

School administrators (and the faculties they supervise) are explicitly commissioned to determine the educational experiences of students. To carry out this charge they are always making selections about the views to which students will be exposed, such as which history texts and novels they'll read, and which explanation for the origin of life they'll learn in science class. Their choices, in turn, must satisfy community standards as represented by school boards and government education departments. If administrators conclude that student leaders are using the school newspaper or other school media to advance positions they find pernicious and which they believe are undermining the moral mission of the school, then they have a responsibility to exert their authority and make the changes they feel are needed.

At the same time, one hopes that administrators will be responsive to students' interests in ideas that may not be mainstream or popular, and use such occasions to launch thoughtful discussions about the ethical and factual bases of those ideas. The goal should not be to suppress ideas, but to make sure that objectionable ideas get challenged.

Chapter 8
PRACTICUM IN MORAL EDUCATION

The Practicum is a workshop designed to provide students with a setting devoted exclusively to discussing moral issues and analyzing their own moral journeys. It should meet one or more times per week and cover a wide variety of moral issues in many different formats (geared, of course, to student ages).

Some of the activities described below involve students sharing personal experiences. Some schools or some individual teachers may not be comfortable with this. Students may become emotional or reveal things that they later regret having disclosed, or that family members may consider private (such as an argument between the child and a parent). While such personal sharing among peers can provide students with a context that may help them better understand their own moral journeys, some schools or teachers may feel these kinds of exercises fall outside of their mandate and expertise as educators, and prefer not to do them.

When schools do include these kinds of exercises, teachers need to set guidelines for student participation. These should include, "What anyone says in the group, stays in the group," "Only share your story if you can do it without revealing the identities of those you interacted with," "No one will be criticized for anything said, not by the teacher and not by fellow students," and "It is not a requirement that students share personal experiences." If a student reveals personal information that the teacher feels is inappropriate, she should ask the student to hold off on telling the rest of the story and meet with him or her privately to discuss her concerns and decide if any further action would be helpful (such as recommending that the student meet with the school psychologist).

ADVISORY PROGRAMS

Some schools have advisory programs that can be used to accomplish the same goals as the practicum course by including some of the exercises described below in their activity list. A guiding principle of advisory programs is to provide students with an adult in the school who gets to know them well, who is there to help and advocate for them, and whose role is not to judge and grade them. In typical advisory programs, advisors meet with small groups of students, informing them about school rules and norms, and working with them on their personal growth and problems they have adjusting to the school's demands and culture (such as in following the rules, or in arranging their study time, or in dealing with peer issues).

The hope is that students will feel more comfortable, more empowered, and more committed to their education by having an adult in the school whose mission is to be on their side, and by developing bonds with fellow group members who are supportive and who are often having similar experiences. A student's comment in an advisory group illustrates the atmosphere that advisors should strive to create. The advisor announced that they were coming to the end of their meeting and the youngster pouted and said she didn't want it to end. The advisor asked why and she replied, "Because I feel so free in here." (For a description and analysis of advisory programs see the book *The Advisory Guide* by Rachel A. Poliner and Carol Miller Lieber, published by Educators for Social Responsibility, Cambridge, MA, 2004; or, for an analysis of the role of the advisor and suggested activities for advisors, see CSEE's *Need a Hand with Advising? Here's a Handbook*, 2004.)

Some advisory programs use exercises that involve the sharing of personal experiences; others feel that this is inappropriate and easily mishandled by teachers who aren't ordinarily trained in this kind of emotional learning. It is worth repeating that if a school uses exercises that elicit personal experiences from students, whether they are doing so in the Practicum in Moral Education course or in an advisory group, students need to be handled sensitively and the guidelines described above should be followed.

Here are some activities that can by used:

MORAL DILEMMA DISCUSSIONS

These may be dilemmas faced frequently by students (such as whether to let a friend copy from your exam, whether to stick up for the class "nerd," whether to exclude an unpopular classmate from your party because a popular classmate says he won't come if the other child is invited, and whether to report a classmate planning to do something mean or destructive). Or the dilemmas may be more hypothetical, such as the kind used by researchers Lawrence Kohlberg (Should a man steal a prohibitively expensive drug that is in short supply in order to save his dying wife?) or Nancy Eisenberg (Should a youngster give up going to a party she has been looking forward to in order to help someone she comes across who is hurt?).

Another kind of dilemma involves serious real-life predicaments, such as those faced by medics on a battlefield who must decide which of the wounded to help first; or by a Catholic Governor trying to reconcile his responsibilities to his Church and his constituents on the issue of abortion; or by a judge faced with the problem of whether to admit illegally obtained evidence in the trial of a murderer who, without it, will assuredly be acquitted.

EVALUATIONS OF CURRENT EVENTS

These may include analyses of current Supreme Court cases and decisions; or the impact of television, films, and recordings on morality; or legal and political philosophies (such as notions of "original intent,""natural law," and "just wars"); or current concerns about medical and corporate ethics; or theories about the causes of crime (Is crime a product of bad people or bad social, political, and economic systems?); or about the impact of the great disparities of wealth in our country (see, for example, Barbara Ehrenreich's *Nickel and Dimed: On (Not) Getting by in America*, Henry Holt and Company, 2001). Every day our newspapers are filled with articles, editorials, and op-eds that can introduce students to the key moral issues of society. (But keep in mind that newspapers and the media, in general, tend to bring us only the bad news. When a government official or corporate executive is incompetent or breaks the law, that's news; when thousands of others do their jobs properly and dutifully, that is not news. In other words, the media, in doing their job of exposing malfeasance and corruption, often give us an overly pessimistic view of human conduct.)

ANALYSES OF MORAL HEROES AND MORAL COURAGE

Students should be presented with stories of moral heroes, both past and present, to learn about their backgrounds and motivations, and to be inspired by them. Christians who saved Jews in Europe during the Holocaust are extraordinary examples of people, many still living, who put their own lives in jeopardy to help others (see *Conscience & Courage* by Eva Fogelman, published by Doubleday Books, 1994, and the film, *The Courage to Care*, distributed by the Anti-Defamation League). Examples of more recent instances of heroism include the black citizens of Los Angeles who risked their lives to rescue whites during the riots after the Rodney King verdict and citizens who tried to save others during the collapse of the World Trade Center buildings. Newspapers and magazines can provide many other examples.

Stories of moral heroes should include individuals who acted alone, in opposition to prevailing community forces (as was the case with many Christian rescuers), and those who found courage within their communities (such as the citizens of Le Chambon in France who collectively rescued thousands of Jews during World War II).

It is also important that students recognize the heroism, not just in eminent figures or those engaged in life and death struggles, but also in the ordinary, day to day lives of many people they know—perhaps even their own parents and neighbors, perhaps even their teachers.

Discussion topics could include the questions of whether there are any background or personality characteristics that are common to moral heroes[9] and whether moral heroes even show consistency within their own characters (Jefferson had slaves, Martin Luther King Jr. has been accused of plagiarism and adultery, Gandhi was purported to have been an insensitive husband). Discussions could also cover how moral courage might be nurtured and what students believe would be worth risking their lives for.

"MORAL" DIARIES/MORAL TURNING POINTS

For this, students would be asked to keep diaries on moral episodes in which they were faced with issues of kindness, fairness, selfishness, guilt, shame, ideals, or any other experience related to their personal morality. They would be asked to record their thoughts and feelings during the incident. The diaries are primarily intended for students' personal use, to help them discover their own moral positions, but students would also be asked to share with the group any experiences they are comfortable talking about.

Students can also write about and discuss moral turning points in their lives. These are experiences that they feel changed the way they think about

9 See, for example, *The Altruistic Personality*, by Samuel Oliner and Pearl Oliner, The Free Press, 1988.

and treat others. One student might report a time he hurt someone and felt so guilty that he resolved never to behave that way again. Another might describe a time she felt ashamed after getting caught doing something she knew was wrong.

Other "feeling" diaries, describing experiences of anger, sadness, love, and happiness, can help students become more aware of what arouses these emotions in them, how they express their feelings, and the impact their feelings have on others (including a discussion of why they might try to hide their feelings from others).

INSPIRATIONAL ART AND WRITING

The goal here is to expose students to art and writing that has explicit moral themes, including stories, plays, and poems (e.g., Charles Dickens' *Nicholas Nickleby*, Mark Twain's *Huckleberry Finn*, George Orwell's *1984*, Jerome Lawrence and Robert E. Lee's *Inherit the Wind*), essays (e.g., Thomas Paine's *The Rights of Man*), films (*High Noon* and *To Kill a Mockingbird* are classics, but there are many others, including many the students will be able to suggest), television shows (*The Simpsons* and *The Cosby Show* are classics but students will have their own favorites), documentaries (e.g. *Eye on the Prize*, *Witness to the Holocaust*), and paintings (Picasso's *Guernica*, Goya's sketches of war). Morally relevant material is available for children of all ages (for example, for younger children, two Dr. Seuss stories, *The Lorax* and *The Sneetches*, have strong moral themes and are entertaining as well).

One purpose is to inspire young people. A second is to get them to analyze the reasoning behind, and implications of, the moral messages. For example, both Charles Dickens and Karl Marx wrote in reaction to appalling economic conditions, but to Dickens the remedy was improved intentions among the rich (a kind of consciousness raising), while to Marx it was the overthrow of capitalism (or system razing). A third purpose is to help students understand the persuasive strategies used by artists so that they are less susceptible to iniquitous and irrational messages.

Discussions should not be limited to "classic" works, but should also cover the moral messages in current popular movies, TV shows, and recordings.

LEARNING "WIN-WIN" NEGOTIATING STRATEGIES

Students can enact real and hypothetical conflicts in order to learn how to seek out solutions that allow both parties to come out ahead. The goal is for them to practice switching from competitive to cooperative conflict-resolution strategies and to recognize that it is in their interest to think beyond their own immediate gain to consider the interests and rights of those they are competing with. The principle is: "Defeat the problem, not the person."

SEXUAL MORALITY

Students need to examine the moral dilemmas inherent in sexual relationships, looking closely at the factors that lead to the dehumanization of people into sexual "objects." Among these are powerful sexual desires, sexual stereotypes and other forms of misinformation about gender and sexuality, feelings of jealousy, traditions of sexual domination and possessiveness, depictions of male-female relationships in terms of "conquests" and similar self-centered constructs, and male-female differences in economic power, intimacy needs, and sexual arousal. Some of these issues can be approached through concrete and practical questions, such as, "How should you treat someone who communicates he or she likes you, but in whom you are not interested?"

A central goal of these discussions should be increased empathy and respect for members of the opposite sex. Discussions should also examine current scientific knowledge about the nature and causes of homosexuality, as well as the plight of homosexuals living in cultures that dehumanize them and regard them as pariahs (while benefiting immeasurably from their creativity).

ANALYZING MORAL CONCEPTS

These can include any concept pertaining to how people treat others. Some examples are friendship, freedom, guilt, altruism, sportsmanship, empathy, love, hate, evil, civil disobedience, race, goodness, loyalty, manners, power, laws, honor codes, and rules, among many others.

Power is a topic of particular interest to young people since they are struggling to move from a position of relative powerlessness to a greater sense of personal control in their social and physical environments. It is important that they understand the difference between destructive power (exemplified by the tough kids on the street corner) and constructive power (exemplified by creative and moral heroes). They need to be reminded that "good guys" (and gals) are not wimps. We don't honor moral heroes because they were easily pushed around or because they went along with the crowd.

Indeed, people who stand strong for their moral beliefs are actually the toughest among us.

One format that some schools have used for teaching children about moral concepts is the "Virtue of the Month." The entire class or school focuses for a month on a single virtue (such as sharing, honesty, or comforting), exploring it both cognitively and experientially. In other words, they analyze the concept, look for instances of it, try to practice it in their daily lives, and discuss their experiences of it with their classmates.

There are a number of published programs that cover a wide collection of virtues (including CSEE's *Creating Classrooms and Homes of Virtue*), but it is worth mentioning that all the common virtues in these programs (with courage and temperance as two exceptions) are derivatives of the central virtues of kindness and fairness. If you intend to be kind and fair, then it follows that you will make an effort to share, to comfort, to be a good sport, and be honest. Courage, when in the service of kindness and fairness, contributes to morality. But courage may also serve immoral ends; some gangsters are courageous. And with regard to temperance, one may be temperate for reasons having nothing to do with kindness and fairness; some temperate people care little about others.

Cultural Institutions and Morality

This refers to the study of the impact of different cultural institutions on the way people treat each other, asking such questions as: How is morality conceived and practiced in different religious, economic, and political systems?

Discussions about morality in different cultures and religions lead naturally to questions about moral relativism: Does one have a right or duty to object to cruel practices in other cultures, or must such practices be accepted simply as their way of doing things? One hopes students will feel a sense of solidarity with, and responsibility for, the downtrodden and victimized anywhere. For example, one hopes they won't consider it moral for women to be treated like chattel, or "untouchables" to be abused, just because it is customary in a particular culture.

Media Projects

Students can use video or audio recordings to explore moral issues, such as taking oral histories of people with handicaps, creating a documentary on the elderly in the community or people who have lived through extraordinary circumstances, such as Holocaust rescuers and survivors, soldiers, recent immigrants, and victims of terrorism. They might also create public service type commercials on moral themes. One documentary could involve interviewing adult family members and friends about the charities they work for or contribute to, exploring why they give their time and money; that is, why they care.

CHARACTER EDUCATION EXERCISES

Teachers can guide students through a variety of character education exercises. Some are designed for groups and some for individuals working independently.

IN YOUR SHOES. This is an empathy exercise in which students imagine themselves in the place of someone they have hurt, imagining what the person is feeling and thinking.

TURN IT AROUND. Students figure out a better solution to real or hypothetical conflicts.

SELF-CONTROL TRAINING. Students imagine themselves faced with some "temptation" and rehearse what to say to themselves to remain faithful to their personal moral standards.

ROLE-PLAYING. Students enact the role of an "adversary" in order to better understand and appreciate his or her perspective.

AM I SOMEONE I LIKE? Students evaluate whether they are living up to their standards—whether they would like themselves if they saw themselves from the outside.

DON'T BECOME WHAT YOU HATE. Students list the characteristics of people they don't like and rate themselves, on a scale from 1 to 10, on these characteristics.

THE GOLDEN CIRCLE. Students verbalize at least one thing they like about each member of the class (and refrain from any negative comments).

WHO NEEDS MY HELP? Students plan how they can benefit a classmate (or, as an alternative, someone in another setting). Perhaps they could try to raise a classmate's self-esteem or improve his or her athletic skills. The next step is to carry out the plan with the assistance of his or her teacher or advisor.

THE FEELING SCORECARD. Students fill out a form that asks on one side, "What have I done to make someone feel good today?" and on the other side, "What have I done that made someone feel bad today?" "And why?"

THE ALIEN TOUR GUIDE. Students enact an improvisation during which some students play "earth-guides" and others play visitors from a distant planet who are interested in learning about some of the good and bad things on earth.

WE'RE ALL CONNECTED. Students explore their connections and indebtedness to others (to the field hand in Central America who picked the banana they had for breakfast, to the mathematicians of ancient Arabia who developed the numeral system they use).

"YES" PEOPLE AND "NO" PEOPLE. Students rank people they know who are prone to say yes to others' requests and those who are prone to say no, and how each makes them feel. Rankings can go from plus five to minus five and students should also rank themselves. Another part of the discussion should consider when it is appropriate to say no, even to friends and family, and the motivations and consequences for those who say yes when they should probably say no (in other words, for people who are easily exploited).

THE TRUTH ABOUT HUMAN NATURE. Students compare the accuracy of pairs of seemingly contradictory "truisms" about human nature, such as, "All people are basically selfish" vs. "It feels good to do good."

I CAN COUNT ON... Students select up to three schoolmates (not necessarily in their own class) whom they feel they can usually count on, and who they believe will stand up for them and will not generally tease, embarrass, or harm them. The selections are kept private, but the names of those selected are then posted.

THE STUDY OF "CARING COMMUNITIES"

In recreating the school as a moral or caring community, it can be both informative and inspiring to study and form psychological bonds to other caring communities, both past and present. Networking and joining forces with other current caring communities (in other schools, in churches, in civic organizations) can increase students' sense of their ability to make "good" things happen.

With regard to "historical" caring communities, among the most extraordinary and dramatic were the communities of Christians who rescued Jews during the Holocaust, risking their own lives and those of their family members to save people who were most often strangers to them. Communities in Le Chambon in France, Assisi in Italy, Neiuwlande in Holland, and Pastor Neimoeller's Confessing Church in Germany can serve as exemplars of moral courage and inspire students with the knowledge that their own caring community is part of a grand human tradition.

LE CHAMBON SUR LIGNON

Le Chambon is a small village and farming community in south-central France. During the four years of Nazi occupation in France, while French collaborators in other parts of the country delivered 75,000 Jews to the Gestapo, the 5,000 residents of the area in and around Le Chambon saved 5,000 Jews who came to them for refuge. Many of the saved were children whose parents had heard about Le Chambon and managed to bring or send their children there.

The guiding spirits of the rescue effort were the local pastor, André Trocmé and his wife, Magda. There was no formal resistance organization in Le Chambon, just a pervasive sense in the community that they would do what was right. Why did they risk their own lives and those of their family members to save outsiders? When interviewed, the rescuers deny that they did anything extraordinary. They did what had to be done, they say. As one citizen put it, "It happened so naturally, we can't understand the fuss."

Some said they helped because of their Christian faith, others because of their hatred of the Nazis, others because of their own history of religious persecution as Protestant Huguenots in Catholic France. All felt a sense of personal responsibility to stand up against evil.[10] Rescuers commonly reported that they did not do a lot of thinking and analyzing before offering aid. As one rescuer expressed it, "The hand of compassion was quicker than the calculus of reason."

ASSISI

Assisi in Italy is the home of the Franciscan order of Catholic monks, devoted to the teachings of St. Francis. In September 1943, Padre Rufino Niccaci, father guardian of the San Diamo Monastery in Assisi was

10 See the film, *Weapons of the Spirit* by Pierre Sauvage, distributed by the Anti-Defamation League, and Philip Hallie's book, *Lest Innocent Blood Be Shed*, Harper & Row, 1979.

summoned to a meeting with Monsignor Giuseppe Placido Nicolini, Bishop of Assisi, and given the dangerous assignment to aid Jews who were seeking shelter in Assisi. The Padre, though an unworldly country friar, managed to find refuge for up to 200 Jews in homes, convents, and monasteries, even arranging Kosher meals for some. He also arranged for false identification papers for all the Jews so they could eventually make their way out of Italy.

Another leader of the rescue effort was Don Aldo Brunacci, a Professor Canon at the San Rufino Cathedral. He hid Jews in cloisters such as the Convent of the Stigmata and also set up a school for Jewish children so they could study their own religious and cultural heritage. There were no attempts at conversion. Father Brunacci was arrested in 1944 but was spared through the intercession of the Vatican upon his agreement to leave Assisi. Later, he recounted, "In all, about 200 Jews had been entrusted to us by divine Providence; with God's help and through the intercession of St. Francis, not one of them fell into the hands of their persecutors." Not one Jew was betrayed in Assisi.[11]

NIEUWLANDE

Nieuwlande is a farm community in Holland that became a rescue center for over 3,000 Dutch Jews. A leader of the operation was Arnold Douwes, who funneled Jews from Amsterdam to the farm of Seine Otten in Nieuwlande. Douwes, who understood the true intentions of the Nazis before many Jews did, frequently exaggerated the comforts and attractions of Nieuwlande in order to convince Jews to leave Amsterdam. He was not against lying to them to save their lives.

The first stop for Jews upon arrival in Nieuwlande was Otten's farm. Then Otten found them hiding places in the community, with families and even with a local minister. Because of the danger, these had to be clandestine operations. To be caught harboring Jews meant death, which was the fate of one of the organizers of the rescue effort, Johannes Post, who was arrested by the Nazis and killed in 1943.[12]

The members of these "caring communities" describe these

11 See A. Ramati's book, *The Assisi Underground: The Priests Who Rescued Jews,* Stein and Day, 1978.

12 See *Rescuers: Portraits of Moral Courage* by Gay Block and Malka Drucker, Holmes and Meier Publishers, 1992.

extraordinary acts of heroism as simply natural responses to people in need. "Well, naturally, come in, come in," they said to terrified Jews who knocked at their doors. Yet attempts at rescue were rare. All across Europe most people turned their backs on the Jews, Gypsies, homosexuals and other targeted groups, or collaborated with the Nazis and turned them in. These rescuers deserve to be heralded and their stories told and retold so the rest of us and the children we bring up and teach can be inspired by their courage.

Today's generation of children needs to learn that even in the most terrifying and disheartening of times, when the darkest aspects of human nature are manifest everywhere, an individual can still choose to live up to the highest standards of compassion and principle.

CHAPTER 9
COOPERATIVE LEARNING

As members of a moral community students need to take responsibility for each other, making sure that all benefit from and enjoy school. Cooperative learning projects in which students help each other and may even be evaluated on their collective product have been found to promote both interpersonal bonds and academic achievement (see *Learning To Cooperate, Cooperating to Learn* by R. Slavin, et al, Plenum Press, 1985).

There are many approaches to cooperative learning but administrators and teachers should keep in mind that cooperativeness is a social skill that can serve both benevolent and malevolent ends. A band of thieves may exhibit high levels of cooperation among members. One can cooperate with others for either moral or practical reasons. The moral ends of cooperative learning programs should be made explicit to students; they are practicing cooperative skills in order to better help others, not simply as a way to increase their own power or competitive advantage by joining forces with others.

Moreover, emphasis should be placed on cooperativeness as a lifestyle, and not merely as an occasionally useful problem solving strategy. In other words, the goal is for students to embrace a more general commitment to seek out mutually beneficial outcomes in all their relationships.

Cooperative learning can take place in various arrangements of two or more students assigned the responsibility to assist each other on a task, such as checking each other's answers on work sheets, or dividing a research project into parts, or brainstorming problem solving strategies. Students' evaluations can be based on the accomplishments of the group as a whole or on a measure of each child's individual contribution to the group or personal level of achievement or amount of improvement.

Be aware that students will often need instruction in the techniques of cooperation. They may not know how to divide up a task, or how to check each other's work and give hints without giving answers, or how to make sure everyone has an opportunity to participate. Teachers will need to monitor the process, not just the product.

Teachers will also need to make sure children find the cooperative activities interesting and the grading fair, otherwise they'll learn a very different lesson from cooperative assignments than the one intended. The goal behind giving students cooperative projects will be undermined if children feel coerced into doing them. If teachers want students to take the cooperative lessons seriously, then they have to model cooperativeness, which begins by being sensitive to students' feelings about the value and fairness of their assignments.

There are some children who don't enjoy cooperative learning. They like to work alone. Some say they think better and are more creative on their own. Others lack the confidence to hold their own in a peer group. Children should learn to work in groups (just as they should learn to work alone), but teachers need to be sensitive to the source of the child's opposition to cooperative projects and help him or her work through it. Certainly a child should not be made to feel that he or she is a bad or inadequate person for resisting cooperative projects.

Also, teachers need to select projects for cooperative learning that are appropriate. I recently heard on the radio a concerto written in China by a committee of composers. It was vapid and predictable, a series of compromises with no driving or coherent vision. Cooperativeness has its limitations. Group brainstorming can lead to creative problem solving, but, in truth, most creative achievements have been produced by lone thinkers, working long and hard on their own.

Regardless of how the cooperative learning projects are structured or evaluated, there are three critical elements that teachers need to emphasize to students in cooperative projects:

BE ENCOURAGING. Help your partners at their own level, providing them with the support they need to improve. Never tease or ridicule or gossip about your partners.

RESPECT EACH PARTNER'S INDIVIDUALITY. Everyone has different strengths and weaknesses, and different interests and information. Do not expect your partners to be like you. Try to appreciate them for who they are.

FULFILL YOUR RESPONSIBILITIES. Recognize that others depend on you and can benefit from your contribution.

CHAPTER *10*
ATHLETICS

There are many opportunities for moral lessons in athletics. In our society, sports usually involve competition (not just recreation)—competition for a place on the team, competition among teammates, and competition between individuals and teams. I don't believe there is anything inherently immoral about competition as long as the contest is run fairly and all competitors enter it voluntarily, knowing that there will be winners and losers. Morality in athletics is concerned with how one competes, not simply with the fact that a competitive event is going on.

Different coaches take different approaches to competition, from "Winning isn't everything; it's the only thing" to "It isn't whether you win or lose, it's how you play the game." The implication of the first statement is that winning is okay even if it is based on cheating. Obviously, if we want our schools to be moral communities, if the quality of life in the community is our main concern, then pride in winning must be based on winning fairly.

Moreover, once students commit themselves to playing fairly, then, in truth, the only thing they have control over is how they play the game. All they can do is play their best and make the game rewarding for everyone by being a good sport. One's best may or may not be good enough to win the game. One can't simply will winning, but one can make an effort to advance one's skills in order to improve one's chances of winning. One can will striving.

Some coaches believe that the only fair approach to children's team sports is for every player to play an equal amount of time, regardless of skill. They feel that this approach will encourage the less skilled youngsters and doesn't leave them sitting on the bench for most of most games. Few would take this approach for school math or chess competitions or in awarding parts for the school musical. In those activities, students with the best math or chess "brains" or best singing and acting abilities are expected to play the central roles. Obviously, in sports, inborn talent, hard work, and strong interest make some players better than others. By everyone getting to play an equal amount of time, those with special abilities may not get the chance to develop their skills to their full potential. They may then miss out on scholarships and even careers that might have been possible for them. Schools should provide all students opportunities to play sports, but in ways that do not impede the growth of those with special abilities.

There are many moral lessons that coaches can provide their players, including:

PLAY FAIR. There is no reason to feel proud if you win by cheating.

DO YOUR BEST. When you enter a competition, for the sake of your own growth, for the sake of your teammates (in team sports), and for the sake of your opponents (to give them an authentic challenge), play hard.

BE A TEAM PLAYER. In team sports, the team is more important than any individual. Play for self-aggrandizement (e.g., hogging the ball) rather than for the benefit of the team is selfish and usually self-defeating—one usually looks bad.

BE ENCOURAGING TO OTHER PLAYERS. Young people frequently mock each other's skills. Often the less skilled players become too worried about making a mistake to play their best or concentrate on the coach's instructions. Many simply give up the game.

APPLAUD GOOD PLAY, even by one's opponents. Athletic excellence is a laudable achievement, usually the result of very hard work. It is worth appreciating and applauding no matter who it comes from.

BE A GOOD SPORT. That means be a gracious winner and a good loser. For example, as a winner one can soften one's opponent's disappointment by pointing out some good plays he made or any improvement you noted in his game. As a loser, congratulating the winner is in order.

CHAPTER 11
TEACHER AND STAFF TRAINING

Because teachers are not always clear about or comfortable with their role in a moral education program, schools should provide appropriate in-service training. Teacher workshops should cover how to make students feel welcomed and safe—psychologically as well as physically—in the school community, how to handle student infractions in ways that promote the development of principles and compassion, how to help students resolve conflicts constructively, and how to empower students in ways that foster their sense of personal responsibility. In other words, teachers should learn how to educate the hearts of their students as well as their minds.

In training teachers to become moral educators the term "community" should be stressed. If we are building a moral community then all students need to feel welcomed and appreciated. Children sense whether they are welcomed by the way teachers look at and greet them, by the supportive, optimistic way teachers help them learn things that are hard for them, by the joy teachers show over their progress, and even by the way teachers criticize them when they break the rules. Many American companies train their personnel to behave in welcoming ways toward the public. It is a learnable skill and there are many teachers who need to learn it.

A welcoming approach will even help when teachers are at a loss at how to handle a child. A teacher who simply blurts out in frustration, "I've had it with you. I'm taking you to the principal," is undermining her own authority. She is admitting defeat and shifting authority to the principal. She is also casting the principal in the role of punisher rather than problem solver. Within the framework of the school as a moral community, when a teacher feels helpless and exasperated, the principal should serve as a resource to help her find a better way to work with the student. In truth, she might simply want to get rid of the child for a while, but in most cases the principal will send him back before long. So it is better to frame taking the child to the principal as an act of problem solving by bringing in additional community resources. The teacher might communicate something like the following (or at least some of it, depending on the circumstance):

> You and I are having a hard time together. I am trying my best to make this class a place where children not only learn a lot but really enjoy learning, but you don't seem to be enjoying it here. And when you misbehave and are disrespectful, I don't enjoy being here, which is very unpleasant for me since I love to teach children. If I'm doing things that make it hard for you to learn or that hurt your feelings, I want you to tell me because that isn't my intention. And I must tell you that when you are disrespectful to me, it hurts my feelings because it says you don't care about me. This is a school where we all strive to make sure that everyone feels cared about, including teachers. I want you to know that if you were trying to learn and another child's behavior interfered with your efforts, I would take action to protect you. I'd do that because that's my job and because I love to see children learning. Now, it is you who are interfering with other children learning so I must protect them from you. So we are going to meet with the principal and tell him about our problem. He's good at helping teachers and students figure out why they aren't getting along and what they can do to make things better. You are important to me so we are going to work this out and come back and have a good class.

This kind of message lets the child know a number of things: that the teacher is firmly in charge of the problem solving process in her class, that the child is still a member of the community that cares about him, that his behavior will not be tolerated for good reasons, and that they and others in the community are engaged in a problem solving process together.

It should go without saying but, unfortunately, it needs to be said: Teachers should never belittle students or make them feel stupid. For instance, some teachers convey to a child that an answer is wrong with an inflection that essentially communicates, "That's wrong, stupid." This, obviously, will discourage most students.

It is also not effective if teachers get into shouting matches with students or any kind of overt power struggle. The more secure teachers are about their authority and abilities, the less likely students will be able to draw them into personal confrontations, even when they get cursed at by a student (which is rare in some schools, but not so rare in others). Teachers are less likely to be thrown by student disrespect and insubordination if they approach each student individually, recognizing that they have to work with the student from the place where he or she starts. If they seek to develop an agenda with each student—a behavioral agenda as well as an academic agenda—then they will view a student's unruliness as a problem to be solved, a problem to which they can apply all their skills and creativity.

One teacher might handle a student's invectives by saying "Cursing is about hurting feelings and that's not what we do here. Take a time out and we'll talk about it later." Another might say "You and I are working together here. If you curse at me it tells me you're giving up and it is important that you don't give up. Let's go back to talking so we can figure out how to solve this problem." When cursed at or challenged, effective teachers convey that they are not shaken by the student's comments, that they are secure in their authority, and that their goal is to find a way to re-engage the student in the learning process. They know they are taking each student on a journey, and with many of their charges it will be a bumpy trip.

Teacher workshops should provide sample dialogues covering what teachers might say to students in a number of the situations they are likely to encounter, as well as the rationales behind the messages. These can be supplemented with improvisations in which teachers play out classroom encounters and get feedback on their effectiveness. Without question, every teacher must develop his or her own style, but the dialogues and improvisations can provide some useful techniques.

For example, the following dialogue between a teacher and a second grader illustrates the technique of "guided imagining," which can teach a lesson that goes beyond simple punishment. The conversation takes place privately in the teacher's office:

TEACHER: Stuart, you took Harry's ball point pen this morning. I told you not to take things from other students' desks. Why'd you take it?

STUART: I don't know. I just wanted it.

TEACHER: We all want things that aren't ours, but everybody has a right to feel safe about their things. I don't want children to have to carry everything around with them all day. And I don't want them to have to worry that their things will be missing when they return. Can you understand that?

STUART: Yes.

TEACHER: What's one of your favorite things?

STUART: My Gameboy.

TEACHER: Close your eyes and imagine that you left it on the desk when you went to Gym. You are coming back now hoping it's where you left it, and it's gone. Picture yourself discovering that it isn't where you left it. See what you'd do and how you'd feel.

STUART: Pretty bad. And I'd get angry at whoever took it.

TEACHER: You might even wonder how someone could be that mean.

STUART: Well, I'd understand why someone would want it. Gameboy is a good toy. But I don't think anyone should just take it.

TEACHER: I don't either. We all want good things, but we can't just take them. Sometimes we can ask someone to get us the thing we want or we can earn the money to buy it ourselves. Now here is an index card that I want you to carry with you. Whenever you see something somebody else has that you really want, I want you to write it down. Then during conference we'll talk about how you might be able to get it. We can even ask your parents if there is a way you can earn some of the things you want. Now I want you to close your eyes again and imagine yourself seeing something you really want on somebody else's desk, say, Harry's pencil. Think how nice it would be to have it, to hold it in your hand. Now imagine that you are about to reach for it. Then imagine that you tell yourself that it is wrong, that the other child will feel terrible and that you know how bad it feels to have something stolen. Tell yourself that you don't want to hurt someone that way and that there are other ways you can try to get it—and that instead of taking it you are going to put it on your list of the things you want.

Not every teacher will be comfortable using guided imagining, or have the time for a lot of one-to-one interaction with students. The technique is not what is important. The important message is that student misbehavior should be responded to in ways that help the student gain self-control based on an understanding of why the behavior is harmful and mean, and what legitimate alternatives might be available to get what he or she is after.

In training, teachers should be reminded that their students' personalities and needs will vary greatly and many will require special sensitivity. One child might be anxious or shy (a "slow to warm up" child) and need time to get used to new people and situations. Another might be desperate for attention and need to be guided into constructive ways to get it. A third might be chronically depressed and need comfort during bouts of sadness. A collaborative approach, with input from school psychologists, guidance counselors, and others who work with the child, can help teachers understand and respond helpfully to their students' special needs. In the same vein, students misbehave for different reasons. One will hit a classmate as a calculated strategy to assert dominance. Another will hit because she feels excluded. The more sensitive teachers are to their students as individuals, the better their chances of coming up with effective interventions for their misbehavior.

One of a school's functions is to help children develop a dependable "work ethic" so they approach their responsibilities with spirit and without griping, and take pride in a job well done. The ethical or interpersonal component of the work ethic involves a willingness to make a contribution to others through one's work. Einstein put it this way:

A hundred times a day I remind myself that my inner and outer life are based on the labors of other men, living and dead, and that I must exert myself in order to give in the same measure as I have received and am still receiving.

School is the work of children and they need to understand that what they learn now prepares them to make a contribution to their communities. In other words, learning has interpersonal or moral implications. This is an important message for teachers to convey, but children will only accept it if they feel that they are in a learning community that cares about them and treats them fairly. Assignments must seem reasonable and examinations fair.

Sometimes children feel that their learning problems are not their own fault, that they are receiving bad or insensitive instruction. And sometimes they are right. Teachers should be open to student comments on their teaching and discuss them without getting defensive. Sometimes simple adaptations will make an enormous difference in student attitudes. Whatever decisions the teacher makes in response to student feedback, and ultimately they are her decisions, she should do her best to explain her reasoning to her students. Simply pulling rank only conveys that the teacher can do whatever she wants because she is in the more powerful position—not a very moral lesson.

As one example of a frequent complaint students have about the instruction they receive is that many teachers don't give them meaningful feedback on their papers, some of which they will have worked on for many weeks. Many teachers just give a grade, a couple of general comments (such as "Very good" or "Good idea, expand"), and perhaps a few punctuation corrections, but no real response to their ideas, no intellectual exchange. If teachers don't have the time to provide meaningful comments on the papers they assign, then they might think about assigning different kinds of papers, such as shorter ones with a narrower focus.

Another kind of problem arises when a child is very committed to learning, but not always to learning what the teacher has assigned. In urging their students toward high standards of learning, teachers need to find a balance that permits them to meet the demands of teaching whole groups while being sensitive to each pupil's individual interests and learning style. This isn't easy, particularly in traditional classrooms in which everyone works on the same assignments at the same pace. Yet there should always be room for some flexibility in assignments to make sure an inquiring mind isn't stifled. In the autobiographies of creative thinkers one finds examples of those who expressed gratitude toward a teacher who recognized and encouraged their individuality, and examples of those who expressed resentment at teachers who tried to shove them into an intellectual box in which they refused to fit.

As teachers, we have a lot to say to students—but we also need to listen to them. The best teaching involves dialogue. Teachers are most effective when they know what the student already knows about the lesson and how he or she is understanding the information provided. But we need to listen to them for another reason. Every child I've ever known, even very young ones, has interesting thoughts and knows things worth hearing about.

Encouraging children to enter into a dialogue with us and conveying that we are interested in what they have to say, is likely to foster their confidence in their thinking processes. It should also increase their motivation to pay attention to what we have to say, even when we are correcting their information and logic.

Respectful dialogue should also be encouraged between students. Teachers can set up open discussions and formal debates on a variety of topics, and teach students the ground rules of respectful discourse (including listening attentively while others speak, confirming that one has understood the other speaker, refraining from personal attacks through words or body language, recognizing other speakers' good points, and keeping the focus on solving the problem under discussion and not getting the better of the other speakers).

TEACHER NETWORKS. These are meetings in which teachers share how they have succeeded or failed in dealing with moral issues in their classrooms, such as teasing, cliques, bullying, and cheating. They can be a fertile source of skills and sensitivities that teachers can pass on to each other.

For example, one gym teacher described how the atmosphere in his classes improved when at the beginning of each semester, instead of merely stating the rules in his usual authoritarian manner, he explained them in terms of respect for others, for their safety, their growth, and their fun. From then on, he tried to phrase all reprimands in terms of how the child's actions failed to treat someone else in the gym with respect. He felt that he was now treating students more respectfully and they were following his example.

A teacher of young children said she found it useful to ask her students at the beginning of the year what kinds of rules the Care Bears would set up if they were in charge of a school. The children came up with very moral rules and adhered to them more readily than they would have if they were simply teacher's rules.

STAFF TRAINING. The welcoming, respectful atmosphere that administrators and teachers seek to create can be undermined if other staff with whom students interact send out contrary messages. Students spend considerable time with bus drivers, office personnel, and cafeteria staff, and administrators should provide guidelines and training to these workers so that they too develop mutually respectful relationships with students. Moreover, since young people can be quite disrespectful to nonacademic employees (who can't give them failing grades or call their parents in for conferences), it is important that these workers feel they have the support of the administration.

Administrators should make sure these staff members feel included in the community. They can do this by treating them respectfully, introducing them at assemblies and describing their contributions to the community, and even having them run periodic tutorials for students, describing how they do their jobs, including the technical requirements of the job and the problem solving tasks they face.

TEACHERS AS MORAL EDUCATORS. There are two important questions that teachers in moral education programs frequently face. The first one pertains to their "credentials": How can teachers, who in their own lives may not be models of morality, teach morality to others? The second, pertains to their "authority": How can teachers lead children toward morality without indoctrinating them?

With regard to whether teachers are sufficiently moral to be entrusted with the task of moral education, the same question could be asked of parents, and clergy as well. If as a society we put off moral instruction until parents and teachers become paragons of virtue, we'd never get to teach morality. Most teachers, like most of our citizens, are pretty decent people, and it is likely that once they begin to teach kindness and fairness to students they will become even better people—more thoughtful and ethical in their own behavior. Parents who take the moral instruction of their children seriously regularly report that, as a byproduct of their concerns for their children, they become more committed to morality in their own lives.

If schools publicly espouse kindness and fairness as instructional goals and have the continuous and open discussions of moral issues advocated here, as well as fairness committees and participatory school governance procedures, individual teachers who don't live up to school standards will not be able to undermine the program. Sufficient structures will be in place to deal with teachers who treat students unfairly or who advocate ethically questionable positions (such as, "Do unto them before they do unto you").

As moral educators, we must accept the fact that in the moral domain most, if not all, of us are less than perfect mortals. Yet, despite our moral imperfections, we are the only ones around to do the job—and we need to get on with it.

Those concerned about indoctrination want students to choose morality, not to be forced or fooled into it. They contend that students must truly understand the options open to them and must commit themselves to moral lives because they believe it is the best path. Otherwise, they argue, the students' commitment to morality will be fragile and undependable, maintained only so long as they are subject to the influence of the moral authorities. These are important considerations.

Indoctrination refers to inducing beliefs through false, misleading, or incomplete information. It is easier to persuade others to your ideology if you give them false "facts" and deceive them about alternative ideologies. You stand a better chance of creating a "good" Nazi by telling lies about Aryans and Jews.

But indoctrination is really not an issue within the framework of morality that I'm recommending. It need not be a concern when one's goals are to foster kindness and fairness. You can't indoctrinate someone to be kind or fair. These are not ideologies. Indeed, they can serve as criteria for the evaluation of ideologies, sensitizing us to which ideologies promote humane values and which advocate hatred and indifference. In actual usage, the term indoctrination implies hatred: to indoctrinate means to demand both allegiance to "our" beliefs and the classification of nonbelievers as enemies to be shunned, converted, or annihilated.

Without question, we want our children to choose kindness and understand its value. But that will happen because we have stimulated the compassionate sides of their natures, not because we have presented them with irrefutable facts or ideologies. One can make a good case for the practical value of treating others well, but one can never prove that kindness and fairness are the most rational ways of living. What criteria could be used in the proof? Kindness and fairness are their own criteria. And as concepts they can be understood by even very young children.

Some teachers will have learned not to expect too much morality from students because morality develops in stages. Theorists like Jean Piaget and Lawrence Kohlberg argued that only older adolescents and adults can reach high moral "stages." But Piaget and Kohlberg were not specifically addressing kindness and fairness. In truth, few studies have found any correlation between these so-called developmental stages and children's or adults' kind or fair actions. Actually, young children can be very kind and fair, more so than many adults. And even very simple children and adults can be kind and fair. It does not require formal education or great intellect.

One of my favorite examples of a "simple" person demonstrating what one might call moral wisdom is of a German man who explained why he risked his life to rescue Jews during World War II:

> I came from a poor family....My mother said to me when we were small, and even when we were bigger, she said to me..."Regardless of what you do with your life, be honest. When it comes the day you have to make a decision, make the right one. It could be a hard one. But even the hard ones should be the right ones." My mother... always in life she gave me so much philosophy. She didn't go to high school... but so smart a woman, wisdom, you know.[13]

The kind of moral "wisdom" this man ascribed to his mother is not the same thing as being "smart" in the ordinary sense of having a high IQ and the ability to engage in sophisticated reasoning and problem solving. There is no correlation between being smart and being kind or fair. Indeed, one can't even prove that it is smart to be kind. This is worth remembering since sometimes people are inclined to yield their moral responsibility to others because they think the others are smarter or know more.

Sophisticated reasoning may enable a kind person to carry out her altruistic intentions more successfully or it may make her more cognizant of the long-term consequences of her acts, but the core precepts of moral action are not very complicated: treat others kindly and fairly, don't harm them, and protect them from harm.

There are certainly dilemmas where it is hard to be sure which action is the most kind or fair, or what one's obligations to others are (Should one tattle on a close friend who has stolen copies of a competitive entrance exam?). Sometimes good reasoning can help us consider and properly evaluate all the relevant information so we don't arrive at illogical conclusions

13 From Perry London's chapter, "The Rescuers: Motivational Hypotheses About Christians Who Saved Jews From Nazis," in L. Macauley and L. Berkowitz' book, *Altruism and Helping Behavior*, Academic Press, 1970.

(such as condemning an entire ethnic group for the misdeeds of a few of its members). But discerning right from wrong (e.g., helping from harming) does not ordinarily require uncommon reasoning skills. Nor is the Golden Rule difficult to grasp. Contrary to Plato's notion of "philosopher kings" and current "stage theories" of moral development, there is no reason to expect better thinkers to be better people; nor are nasty people particularly likely to be dumb.

Freud too believed that children were incapable of morality—that conscience, or what he called the "super ego," did not emerge until the child was about seven, and only if conditions were right, and only, oddly, in males. His theory was not at all based on the observation of children and, whatever its merits in other areas, it was simply wrong about conscience development.

Another questionable theory that teachers will come across argues that the reason adolescents don't exert self-control is because their brains haven't developed sufficiently. But, look around. Many adolescents exert a great deal of self-control and are able to multitask and plan for the future. Many do hours of homework after hours of school, where they study five or six different subjects. And then they take music lessons, and work on SAT preparation materials, and play sports and computer games, among other activities. In many cultures adolescents are expected to exert self-control and they do. I've worked with adolescents who got into serious trouble until their eighteenth birthday, and then stopped abruptly. When I asked them why they stopped, the said because now they could go to jail for those behaviors. Nothing changed in their brain circuitry on their eighteenth birthday.

As a psychologist, I'd also recommend that teachers be wary of psychological or psychiatric diagnostic labels placed on children, like "disruptive behavior disorder," "conduct disorder," and "oppositional defiant disorder." They are only technical sounding ways of describing the child's misbehavior. They tell us nothing about the causes of the child's behavior, nothing intrinsic about the child, nothing about his or her potential.

Our children come into the world with the capacity to become kind and fair. We will help that occur by setting up the conditions that make kindness and fairness feel good to them so goodness becomes its own reward.

CHAPTER 12
PARENT INVOLVEMENT

Recognizing the primacy of parents in moral instruction, parents need to be brought into the program. In various settings, such as workshops, lectures, and counseling sessions, parents can be provided with ways they can support their child's moral, social, and academic development. A child in the type of program described here will have lots on her mind that she will want to discuss with her parents. In meetings with parents, teachers can help prepare them for the kinds of moral issues their children will bring up.

There is substantial evidence for the benefits—both academic and behavioral—of parents taking an active role in monitoring their child's education and in working closely with the school. It sends a clear message to the child that the most important adults in his life, his parents and teachers, take his school life very seriously.

Moreover, sometimes a parent's moral lessons conflict directly with the school's, as when a parent instructs a child to "Never tattle but always hit back," while the teacher insists, "Don't hit back; come and tell me." Clearly, the teacher needs to explain the reasons for her rules and convey to the parent that in school the child must adhere to school rules.

While parent involvement is certainly to be encouraged, a number of experienced teachers have made the same comment to me about how parents have changed over the years. In their early years as teachers, when they called a parent to school to discuss his or her child's misbehavior, the parent was almost always cooperative, eager to work with the teacher to improve the child's behavior. Now, though, they find that many parents are defensive, frequently less concerned about the child's behavior than what will go on his or her "permanent" record. Some parents have even threatened legal action to keep an incident off their child's record. These teachers expressed their disappointment that parents today worry more about their child getting into the "best" prep school or college than about his or her character.

I believe that as parents become more integrated into the school, more involved themselves in discussions of values and how the school can foster them, this kind of parental alienation becomes less likely. Indeed, the parents' own commitment to moral values and to bringing up moral children will be strengthened as they become increasingly involved in helping recreate the school as a moral community.

Parents often become cynical about teaching their children to care about others. They worry about their child being the only one who isn't grabbing all he can as quickly as he can. It is reassuring for parents to meet other parents with the same values and concerns, to learn that they are not the only ones who care about moral issues and their children's character.

When I speak to parent groups I often ask them for a show of hands on how many have watched the movie, *It's a Wonderful Life*, many times or even every year. Many raise their hands. I then ask how many have introduced their children to the film. Again, many hands go up. I ask them to look around at all the hands that are raised.

The message of that movie is a reply to cynicism. It says that a wonderful life is a life of helping others. I point out that while they sit home watching the movie, moved to joy and tears yet grumbling about how no one cares, their neighbors across the hall and across the country are watching the same film for the same renewal—believing in the same inspiring message. Through parent groups, the school can help parents discover that there are others who share their values and who will work with them to create a more caring community.

There are various ways parents can be brought more fully into the school community. For instance, the school can offer parenting workshops on major childrearing issues that bear on school performance, covering such diverse topics as how to foster empathy in children and how to get them to take responsibility for their homework.

Schools can also communicate more with parents about their activities and programs. For example, they could let parents know which moral issues are being examined so parents and children can discuss these issues at home. Schools would also do well by letting parents know when their children behave kindly or fairly. Too often schools communicate only the bad news, such as that a child is fighting or cheating. When schools inform parents of their child's "good" behavior, parents can reinforce the behavior with recognition and praise.

In working with parents, schools might do well to remind them that being a kid is not always easy. At any age, but especially during their teen years, most students (like most adults) want to make their own choices, including choosing their own companions, clothing styles, and daily routines. And teens most definitely want to be able to pursue their romantic and sexual desires, and anything else that they believe will bring them pleasure. These are not unnatural impulses, nor are they inherently immoral. In truth, our species did not evolve for young people to sit in classes all day and do home work all night. Nor did we evolve for teens to be parented. In earlier eras (and in certain societies even today) teens took their places as full-fledged members of the community, starting their own families and making their own livings. In modern societies, too often, we treat teens as big children, constantly telling them what to do, when to do it, and with whom to do it. Just at the time when we feel they need our guidance more than ever, they are demanding, frequently screaming for, more autonomy—so we should not be surprised when friction arises between us and them. Parents who have good relationships with their children, especially during the teen years, manage to convey to their kids that they are truly on their side, that they can understand and take pleasure in their passions, and that they will attempt to restrict them only when they feel certain that their actions will lead to harm for themselves or others.

CHAPTER *13*

THE SCHOOL AND SOCIAL PROBLEMS:
SEX, ALCOHOL AND DRUG EDUCATION

Many school systems have introduced sex, alcohol, and drug education programs, often under pressure from community groups and political leaders who are hoping the schools can succeed where families and churches have failed.

These are difficult areas and too often we confuse our students by failing to help them differentiate among the moral, the legal, the conventional, the personal, and the health aspects of sexual behavior and alcohol and drug use. Schools should certainly cover the health aspects, such as the effects of alcohol and drugs on the mind and body, information about pregnancy and birth control, and the nature and risks of sexually transmitted diseases. The insidious nature of alcohol and drug addiction is particularly important for young people to understand since during their early experimentation with addictive substances many feel that they couldn't possibly develop a dependency.

Schools should also provide forceful instruction about the interpersonal or moral implications of these health issues, such as the profound responsibility that comes with bringing children into the world, the absolute obligation to avoid transmitting sexual diseases, and the devastating impact of drug and alcohol use on one's ability to meet one's social responsibilities (such as when driving a car or doing one's job or playing on a team).

The impact of drug and alcohol use on the quality of life in the community should also be discussed but it is a more complex subject in which one must try strike a balance between moral concerns (e.g., how does an individual's drug or alcohol use affect others?), legal questions (e.g., what is a proper consequence for those who violate drug and alcohol laws), and personal rights (e.g., does anyone have a right to tell me what I can put into my own body?). One might, for example, ask whether there are any acceptable levels of drug or alcohol use, and if there are, how do individuals and communities determine those levels? Also, would legalizing drugs reduce the disorderliness and crime in our communities, or, rather, speed their decay and make them even more violent?

Individual teachers may have views on these questions and they should be matters for open debate, but I believe it would be a mistake for a school to adopt a policy on these issues ("Bring back prohibition," "Legalize marijuana") that all teachers and students are expected to echo.

Similarly, I believe it would be a mistake for schools to adopt positions on what kinds of sexual contact their students should and shouldn't engage in at what ages (None before marriage? Kissing at fourteen? Petting at sixteen?). These are matters of community convention, and, though important, are not in the same category as moral matters that concern intentionally harming or helping others.

This is not to say that moral considerations do not enter into sexual relationships. Without question they do. One can be abusive or exploitative in sexual relationships as well as any other relationships, and, as mentioned earlier, the entire topic of male-female relationships, including sex, is an important moral area to explore with students. But parent or teacher judgments about which sexual activities are appropriate for youngsters at what ages are usually based more on social and religious traditions than reasoned evaluations of whether they are harmful or helpful to particular individuals in particular contexts.

We need to recognize that social practices are ever evolving and that our society has gone through a significant change in sexual mores during recent decades. Young people are having sex at younger ages and with more partners than earlier generations. Some educators and psychologists warn that premarital sex during the teenage years has terrible psychological consequences and they offer anecdotes of youngsters who became depressed or mentally disturbed in other ways as a result of their sexual experiences.

Actually, there is no evidence that any substantial number of teenagers who engage in premarital sex are harmed by their experiences. Just as there are particular individuals who regretted and felt damaged by their teenage sexual encounters, there are others who felt it did not harm them in any way or that their lives were enriched by their sexual experiences. My advice is to be wary of "experts" who warn of dire psychological "health" risks to teenagers who engage in sex. They usually have a hidden agenda, a religious agenda. They use the rhetoric of "health" but, in fact, are against sex outside of marriage because they consider it immoral. But for many now the judgment of whether someone is a moral person is not based on the simple fact of whether or not he or she has had premarital sex, or whether he or she has engaged in homosexual sexual activity. Obviously, exploitative and abusive sex acts, such as sexual harassment, rape, adultery, and sex with a child, are immoral. But it is not hard to find kind and fair teenagers who are engaging in sex, and mean ones who aren't.

If schools take on the responsibility of educating about sex and alcohol, they need to help students distinguish between the moral, the legal, the conventional, the personal, and the health aspects of these behaviors. As one example of educating about the moral implications of sexual behavior, schools could provide a workshop in sexual harassment (including harassment of homosexuals), covering school rules and laws about unwanted sexual comments and advances, as well as the impact these have on their targets and on the community at large.

In general, as moral educators, we should resist trying to force students to accept simple solutions (such as abstinence is the best way) to complex issues. And we should never try to control them by mislabeling conventional sexual issues (such as what kind of sexual contact is okay at what age under what circumstances) as health or moral issues (say, by arguing that people who are sexually abstinent except in marital relationships are somehow more noble or healthful than those who are not). We will lose their trust if we do.

Some schools have introduced programs to help students resist peer pressure to engage in sex or use alcohol and drugs when they would rather not. Sometimes students fear ostracism or ridicule if they don't go along with the crowd. These students could benefit from social skills training which schools can provide in special workshops and counseling sessions (perhaps in the practicum course or in advisory groups). These programs should give students a better understanding of their rights in a friendship, as well as practice in refusal skills. Some students may also need to learn more about how to make friends so they won't feel so dependent upon false friends who try to manipulate and seduce them into doing things they'd rather not do.

CHAPTER 14

THE SCHOOL AND THE COMMUNITY

Eventually our students will take their place as adults in the community and we need to prepare them by teaching them as much as we can about how the community operates, about its politics and problems, about how people earn their livings and how wealth is distributed. Many high school seniors have already reached the voting age of 18. They need to know the ways their community enhances citizens' lives (from protection from enemies to senior centers to restaurant cleanliness inspections), and also about citizen dissatisfactions and discontent. Of great importance, they need to know the procedures available for making the community better.

These areas can be addressed in regularly scheduled community forums (with invited speakers when appropriate), and by "research" excursions to various places in the community (such as the courthouse and the city council). Students should be introduced to a broad array of political views about local and national public issues, such as rent control, environmental impact, and minimum wage laws.

Some community issues directly involve the school and students should be encouraged to think about and talk about the link between school and community. For example, some schools are located in poor, violent communities in which drug gangs control the streets. What can the school offer students in such a community? Perhaps a sanctuary. Perhaps the only place that they can experience kindness, fairness, and stability. Perhaps a vision of a better world that they can truly aspire toward. Perhaps a mini-course on urban architecture and aesthetics can have an impact on the way youngsters think about graffiti and vandalism.

Many public schools are rundown, with inadequate teaching facilities and supplies. What does that tell students about the commitment of the community toward education? Sometimes teachers work in communities in which they cannot afford to live, teaching students who are in danger of defining themselves in terms of what they own, sometimes teaching students who drive their own luxury cars to school while their parents on the Board vote down teacher requests for a better health plan. What impact might this have on the teachers' sense of community?

There are many such issues that arise and they should be aired in a community forum or the practicum class. In addition, students should be made aware of the broader community power structure in which the school is embedded. If students are to effectively participate in recreating their school as a moral community they must understand the political, social, and economic forces acting on the school, such as how funding happens, what role teachers (and, when relevant, their union) play in making school policy, and what social class and racial issues are at play. This kind of understanding not only makes them aware of the obstacles to making their school and community better, but also gives them an appreciation of the devoted efforts that many in the community make to improve their fellow citizens' lives.

AFTERWORD
SCHOOLS AND THE MEANINGFUL LIFE

People who experience their lives as meaningful have something in common. They feel that they are connected to something larger than themselves, something that gives unity and purpose to their countless actions. This connection, whatever it is, helps them deal with the inevitable ups and downs of existence and provides some solace for the fact that they, their loved ones, and everyone one they know will eventually die.

Some people find meaning through their religion; others through their commitment to some grand social philosophy or "ism." Religions and "isms" offer adherents a pre-formed structure that tells them what life is about and how they should live it. Those without such overarching schemas must struggle to construct a meaningful life on their own. Schools can help.

As they often describe it, those who experience their lives as meaningful see themselves as embedded in a continuity of human experience, connected, not only to those around them, but to those who lived before them and those who will live after they are gone. Frequently they feel indebted to those in the past whose efforts they have benefited from, and they feel a responsibility toward those whose lives their life will affect. Their sense that so much good was created by others before them and passed on to them, makes them feel beholden to continue the process and create and pass on good to others, to those they interact with and, ultimately, to those who will come after them.

Schools can play a role in helping students find meaning in their lives. They can do it by making clear that everything they teach, whether about the glories of human achievement or the follies that led people down dark paths, was selected to help students figure out their own place in the flow of human history and how they too can create and pass on good things.

INDEX

ABOUT THE AUTHOR

MICHAEL SCHULMAN, PH.D., is the author of *Bringing Up a Moral Child: A New Approach for Teaching Your Child To Be Kind, Just, and Responsible* (Addison-Wesley, 1985; revised edition, Doubleday Books, 1994), *The Passionate Mind: Bringing Up an Intelligent and Creative Child* (The Free Press, 1991; a Book-of-the-Month Club selection), and chapters on the development of moral motivation and intelligence in *The Handbook of Positive Psychology* (edited by C. R. Snyder and Shane J. Lopez; Oxford University Press, 2002). He has also written professional and popular articles on childrearing, psychotherapy, and antisocial behavior, including articles for *Parents* and *Working Mother* magazines and the "FamilyTalk" column in the newspaper *Her NY*. He has been a featured guest on many major television and radio talk shows (Oprah, Sally Jessy Rafael, The CBS Morning Show, among others), speaking about moral education and creativity.

Dr. Schulman is chairman of the Columbia University Seminar on Ethics, Moral Education, and Society and is a psychologist for Leake & Watts, a child care agency, where he incorporates "moral motivation" procedures into his clinical work with inner city adolescents in residential treatment. He has also consulted for public and private schools on introducing values education programs into their curricula, and was the Director of Ethical Education for the Ethical Culture Society of Queens, N.Y. His approach to the prevention of antisocial behavior is described in his chapter, "The Prevention of Antisocial Behavior Through Moral Motivation Training (or Why Isn't There More Street Crime?)," in the book, *Protecting the Children* (edited by Raymond Lorion; Haworth Press, 1990). He has also been an advisor to public and private television production companies on values education programming.

Dr. Schulman has taught psychology at Yeshiva University's Ferkauf Graduate School of Psychology and at Rutgers University, Fordham University, and Hunter College. He has also been an acting teacher, director, and playwright, and has authored a number of widely read books and articles on theatre and acting.